Contents

Features

The *Maps: Read, Understand, Apply* series has been developed to teach important geography and social studies skills in four levels. Up-to-date, in-depth information in a self-contained format makes this series an ideal resource. Clear, concise maps present new concepts in a straightforward manner without overwhelming students. As students develop practical skills, such as map interpretation, they also develop the confidence to use these skills. The features incorporated into the series were developed to achieve these goals.

Two books make up the series:
Maps: Read, Understand, Apply, Grades 3–4
Maps: Read, Understand, Apply, Grades 5–6

Each book in the series is organized into four units. All units include a combination of teaching pages that introduce the skill and include practice pages, a review, and an application activity.

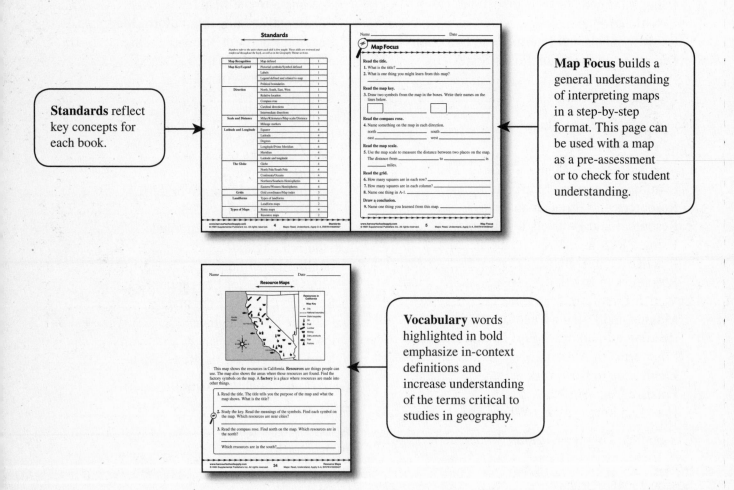

Standards reflect key concepts for each book.

Map Focus builds a general understanding of interpreting maps in a step-by-step format. This page can be used with a map as a pre-assessment or to check for student understanding.

Vocabulary words highlighted in bold emphasize in-context definitions and increase understanding of the terms critical to studies in geography.

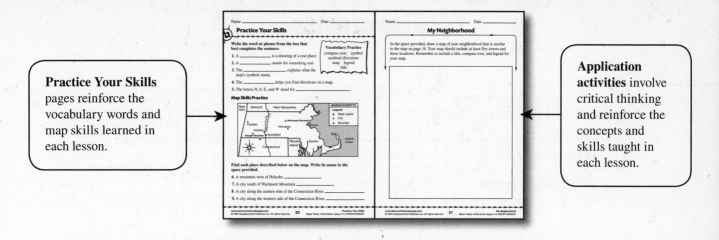

Practice Your Skills pages reinforce the vocabulary words and map skills learned in each lesson.

Application activities involve critical thinking and reinforce the concepts and skills taught in each lesson.

Introduction to Geography introduces the five themes of geography at the beginning of the book. This four-page feature provides definitions and questions that encourage students to think about the broad aspects of each theme.

Geography Theme sections further explain the five themes of Geography. Each four-page section emphasizes the concepts and the relevance of the theme.

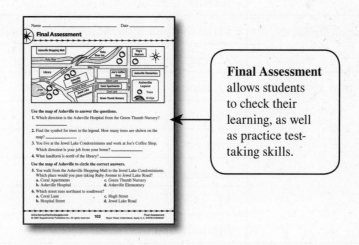

Final Assessment allows students to check their learning, as well as practice test-taking skills.

Atlas maps are a valuable reference tool for instruction and study.

The **Glossary** serves as both an index and a resource for definitions of key terms.

Standards

←——————————————————————→

Numbers refer to the units where each skill is first taught. These skills are reviewed and reinforced throughout the book, as well as in the Geography Theme sections.

Map Recognition	Map defined	1
Map Key/Legend	Pictorial symbols/Symbol defined	1
	Labels	1
	Legend defined and related to map	1
	Political boundaries	1
Direction	North, South, East, West	1
	Relative location	1
	Compass rose	1
	Cardinal directions	1
	Intermediate directions	1
Scale and Distance	Miles/Kilometers/Map scale/Distance	3
	Mileage markers	3
Latitude and Longitude	Equator	4
	Latitude	4
	Degrees	4
	Longitude/Prime Meridian	4
	Meridian	4
	Latitude and longitude	4
The Globe	Globe	4
	North Pole/South Pole	4
	Continents/Oceans	4
	Northern/Southern Hemispheres	4
	Eastern/Western Hemispheres	4
Grids	Grid coordinates/Map index	3
Landforms	Types of landforms	2
	Landform maps	2
Types of Maps	Route maps	4
	Resource maps	2

→→→→→→→→→→→→→→→→→→→→→→→→→→→→→→→→→→→→

www.harcourtschoolsupply.com
© HMH Supplemental Publishers Inc. All rights reserved.

4

Standards
Maps: Read, Understand, Apply 3–4, SV9781419099427

Name _____ Date _____

Map Focus

➤➤➤➤➤➤➤➤➤➤➤➤➤➤➤➤➤➤➤➤➤➤➤➤➤➤➤➤➤

Read the title.

1. What is the title? _____

2. What is one thing you might learn from this map?

_____

Read the map key.

3. Draw two symbols from the map in the boxes. Write their names on the lines below.

☐ _____   ☐ _____

Read the compass rose.

4. Name something on the map in each direction.

north _____   south _____

east _____   west _____

Read the map scale.

5. Use the map scale to measure the distance between two places on the map.

The distance from _____ to _____ is

_____ miles.

Read the grid.

6. How many squares are in each row? _____

7. How many squares are in each column? _____

8. Name one thing in A-1. _____

Draw a conclusion.

9. Name one thing you learned from this map. _____

_____

➤➤➤➤➤➤➤➤➤➤➤➤➤➤➤➤➤➤➤➤➤➤➤➤➤➤➤➤➤

Maps: Read, Understand, Apply 3–4, SV9781419099427

Name _____   Date _____

Introduction to Geography

In *Maps: Read, Understand, Apply* you will learn about some of the tools that scientists use to study **geography.** Geography is the study of Earth and the ways people live and work on Earth. Scientists use five themes, or main ideas, to help them organize information as they study geography.

The Five Themes of Geography
- Location
- Place
- Human/Environment Interaction
- Movement
- Regions

Geography Themes

⊙ **Location** is where something can be found. One way to describe the location of something is by using numbers and a street name, or an address. Another way is by telling what the location is near.

Think about your home. Where is it located? What is it near? Think about the numbers and street name that make up your address.

1. Kareem lives in this house. Tell the location of his house.

⊙ **Place** describes a location. Place tells about the **physical features** formed by nature, such as bodies of water, landforms, climate, and **natural resources.** Natural resources are things from nature that people can use. Some natural resources are trees, oil, and gold. Place also tells about the location's **human features,** or features made by people. Some examples of human features are buildings, roads, farms, schools, and shopping malls.

These illustrations show two places. The first illustration shows the city of St. Louis. The other illustration shows Yosemite National Park.

2. What is one human feature of St. Louis?

_____

3. What is one physical feature of Yosemite National Park?

_____

⊙ **Human/Environment Interaction** explains how people live in their environment. **Environment** is the land, water, and air around you. It is the plant and animal life, too. How people make a living often depends on their environment. For example, people who live near the sea might fish for a living.

4. How might living on the plains be different from living in the mountains?

_____

_____

_____

Human/Environment Interaction also describes how people live in their environment by changing it. People might cut down trees to clear the land and build offices and other buildings.

5. Look at the illustrations shown here. Why have people changed the environment in these places?

_____

_____

_____

⊙ **Movement** describes how people, goods, information, and ideas move from place to place. Movement happens through transportation and communication.

People move in cars, buses, ships, trains, and planes. What are some ways goods move from place to place?

Information and ideas also move from place to place. This happens through newspapers and magazines, by computer and telephone, and on radio and television.

6. How are information and ideas moving in this picture?

_____

⦿ **Regions** are areas that share one or more features. A physical feature can describe a region. The Ohio River Valley is a physical landform region described by the Ohio River. A human feature, such as how the land is used, can also describe a region. Coal mining areas, such as those found in West Virginia and Kentucky, form human land use regions because the land is used to mine natural resources. Regions can be as large as your state or as small as your neighborhood.

7. The Rocky Mountains run through Canada and the United States for more than 3,000 miles. What do you think makes the Rocky Mountains a region?

_____

_____

_____

9

Name _____   Date _____

Geography Theme: Movement

Movement explains how people, goods, and ideas get from one place to another. Movement also tells how people in a community depend on people in other communities for goods and services.

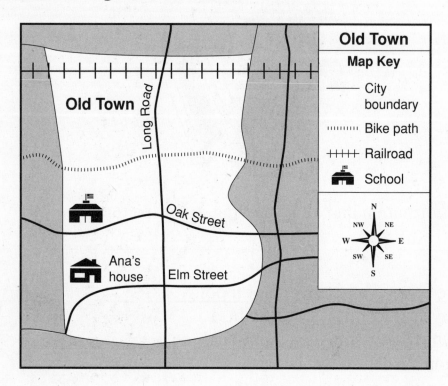

1. The map above shows Old Town, where Ana and her family live. Find Ana's house on the map and circle it.

2. Name three kinds of transportation routes in Old Town.

   _____

3. What streets would Ana's mother take to drive her to school?

   _____

4. Ana's family likes to ride on the bike path. What streets does the family take to get to the bike path from Ana's house?

   _____

Maps: Read, Understand, Apply 3–4, SV9781419099427

Name _____ Date _____

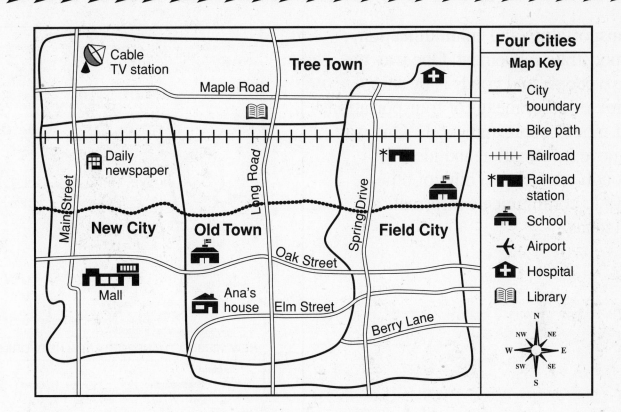

1. In which community can Ana shop at stores?

_____

2. Name two ways ideas move in these communities.

_____

3. Where can Ana and her family go to get on the train?

_____

4. The people in the four communities want an airport. Draw a symbol on the map where you would put the airport. Write why this would be a good place to build an airport.

_____

_____

Name _____ Date _____

Transportation and communication demonstrate movement. One way to move people and goods is by ship. Think of other means of transportation that move people and goods. One way to move information and ideas is through television. Think of other ways to communicate information and ideas.

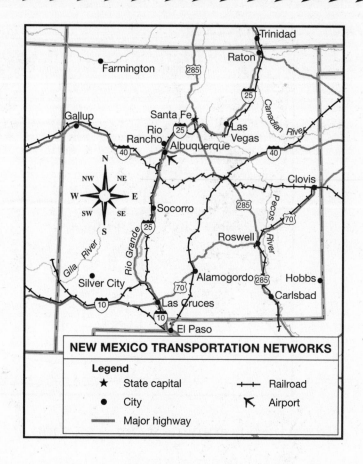

NEW MEXICO TRANSPORTATION NETWORKS

Legend
★ State capital   ┼┼┼ Railroad
● City   ✈ Airport
━━ Major highway

1. What are two ways to move goods and people from Carlsbad to Clovis?

_____

2. What city is the center of transportation in New Mexico? Why do you think this is so?

_____

_____

3. Trace the shortest driving route from Las Cruces to Santa Fe. What highway would you take from Las Cruces to Santa Fe?

_____

4. What cities would you pass through between Las Cruces and Santa Fe?

_____

Name _____ Date _____

Ideas and information can be moved from place to place. For instance, information about current events can be found in a newspaper or on television or radio. Books are another way to learn about things.

Look at the ways people learn about ideas and information. Write the letter of the picture or pictures that show where information can be found.

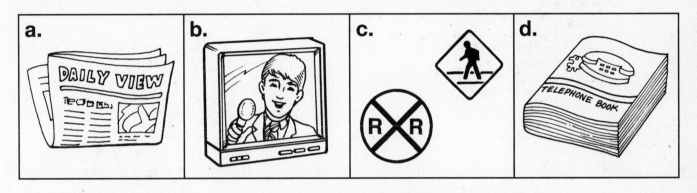

_____ **1.** Luis wonders who won last night's basketball game.

_____ **2.** Jill wants to know what happened at the city council meeting.

_____ **3.** Mike needs to know the address of a restaurant.

_____ **4.** Kim is watching for a building across from the railroad crossing.

_____ **5.** Mr. Reyna is looking for someone to mow his yard.

_____ **6.** Lisa can't decide if she should wear her winter coat.

_____ **7.** Kara wants to call a new friend, but she needs the phone number.

_____ **8.** Miss Hotz remembers to slow down her car near a crosswalk.

_____ **9.** Jim wants to find a new job.

_____ **10.** Omar needs the phone number of a doctor.

Geography Theme: Movement
Maps: Read, Understand, Apply 3–4, SV9781419099427

Name _____ Date _____

Directions and Legends

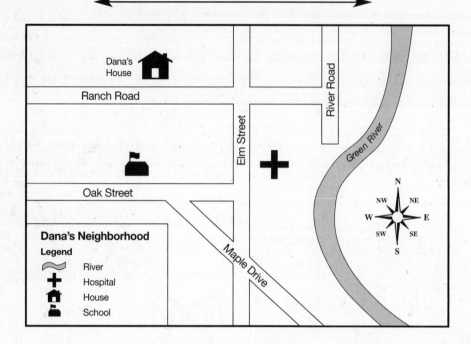

A **map** is a drawing of a real place. A map shows the place from above. The map above shows Dana's neighborhood. Use the map to find Dana's house. What other things does the map show?

Follow these steps to begin reading a map.

1. Read the title of the map. The **title** tells you what the map is about. What is the title of the map on this page?

_____

2. Read the legend. The **legend,** or **map key,** tells you what each map **symbol** stands for. Match each symbol in the legend to a symbol on the map. Name two places using symbols on the map.

_____

3. Read the compass rose. The **compass rose** helps you find directions. The arrows pointing to north (N), south (S), east (E), and west (W) are the four **cardinal directions.** Name places on the map that are north, south, east, and west of the hospital.

_____

_____

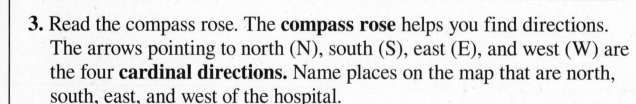

Maps: Read, Understand, Apply 3–4, SV9781419099427

Name _____   Date _____

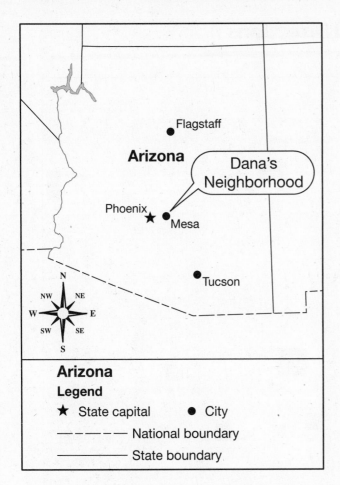

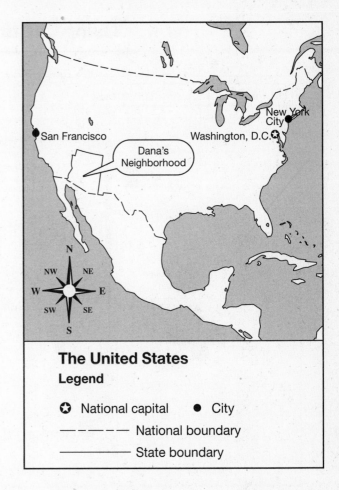

Dana's neighborhood is in the city of Mesa. Mesa is in the state of Arizona. The map on the left shows the state of Arizona. Find Dana's city on the map.

Arizona is in a country, the United States. The map on the right shows the United States. Find Dana's state, Arizona.

You can see that Dana lives in a neighborhood, a city, a state, and a country all at the same time.

Answer these questions about the map of Arizona. Use the legend and the compass rose.

1. Is Mesa east or west of Phoenix? _____

2. Is the state capital north or south of Flagstaff? _____

Answer these questions about the map of the United States. Use the legend and the compass rose.

3. Is New York City north or south of Washington, D.C.? _____

4. Is Arizona east or west of the national capital? _____

Name _____ Date _____

Using Cardinal Directions

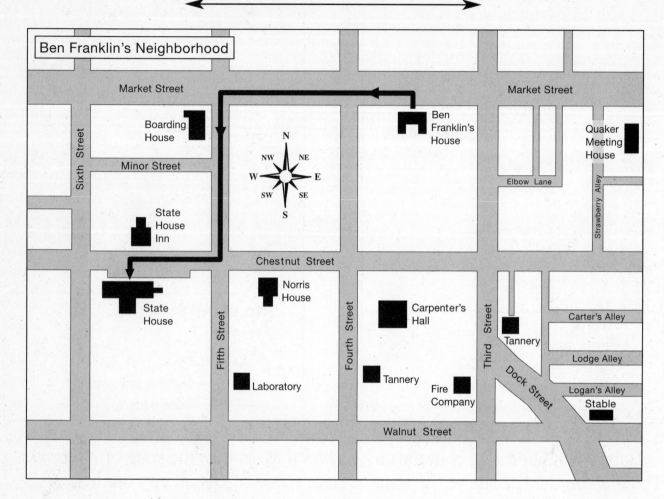

Ben Franklin's Neighborhood

1. Read the title. Write it here.

_____

2. Read the compass rose. Circle the north arrow.

3. What direction would you travel moving from the Boarding House to the State House? _____

4. What direction would you travel moving from the Tannery to Ben Franklin's House? _____

5. What place is located east of Fifth Street and west of Fourth Street?

_____

6. What place is located north of Carpenter's Hall? _____

Maps: Read, Understand, Apply 3–4, SV9781419099427

Name _____ Date _____

Using Symbols and Directions

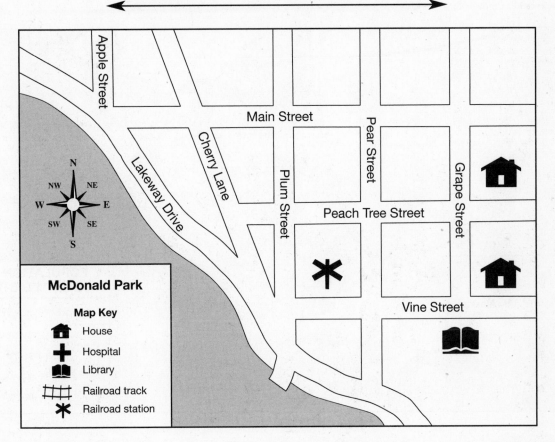

1. Read the title. Write it here.

   _____

2. Read the map key: Check (✔) each symbol after you read its meaning.
   Check (✔) a matching symbol on the map.

3. Read the compass rose. Circle the north arrow.

Finish the map by adding these symbols.

4. Draw a hospital north of Main Street between Plum Street and Pear Street.

5. Draw a house south of Peach Tree Street between Pear Street and Grape Street.

6. Draw a house east of Apple Street and north of Main Street.

7. Draw a railroad track down Plum Street, from north to south.

8. Draw a house west of Cherry Lane and south of Main Street.

Maps: Read, Understand, Apply 3–4, SV9781419099427

Name _____ Date _____

Reading a Population Map

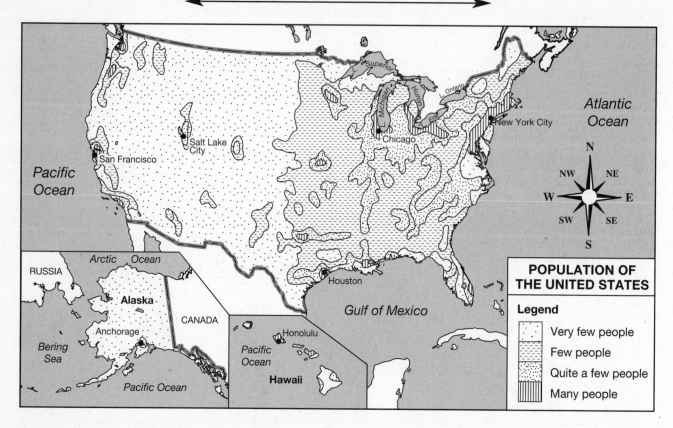

Population is the number of people who live in a place. Look at the population map above. It shows you how many people live in different areas of the United States.

1. Which pattern shows that many people live in an area? Draw that pattern on the line.

   _____

2. Which city has more people living there: Salt Lake City or San Francisco?

   _____

3. Find Houston on the map. Do <u>many</u> or <u>very few</u> people live there?

   _____

4. Find Chicago on the map. Do <u>many</u> or <u>few</u> people live there?

   _____

5. Why do you think people want to live in these areas of the United States?

   _____

Name _____ Date _____

Reading Symbols on a Map

←————————————————————→

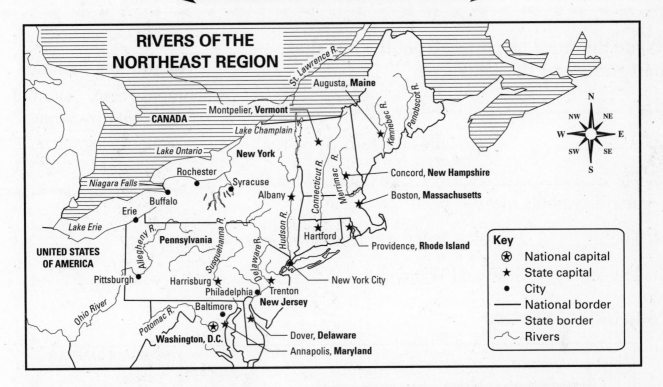

RIVERS OF THE NORTHEAST REGION

St. Lawrence R.
Augusta, **Maine**
Montpelier, **Vermont**
CANADA
Lake Champlain
Lake Ontario
New York
Rochester
Niagara Falls
Syracuse
Buffalo
Albany
Erie
Lake Erie
Allegheny R.
Pennsylvania
Susquehanna R.
Hudson R.
Connecticut R.
Merrimac R.
Kennebec R.
Penobscot R.
Concord, **New Hampshire**
Boston, **Massachusetts**
Hartford
Providence, **Rhode Island**
UNITED STATES OF AMERICA
Pittsburgh
Harrisburg
Philadelphia
Ohio River
Potomac R.
Baltimore
Trenton
Delaware R.
New Jersey
New York City
Washington, D.C.
Dover, **Delaware**
Annapolis, **Maryland**

N
NW   NE
W   E
SW   SE
S

Key
⊛ National capital
★ State capital
• City
— National border
— State border
⌇ Rivers

The map above shows the rivers in the Northeastern region of the United States. If you look closely at the map, you'll find the symbol in the map key that represents rivers. Notice that each river is labeled on the map with its name.

1. Which river flows through Concord, New Hampshire?

_____

2. Name the national capital of the United States.

_____

3. What city is south of Niagara Falls?

_____

4. What two countries does the national border separate?

_____

5. What state does the Kennebec River flow through?

_____

6. Name the river that flows southward through Albany and New York City.

_____

➤➤➤➤➤➤➤➤➤➤➤➤➤➤➤➤➤➤➤➤➤➤➤➤➤➤➤

Name _____   Date _____

Practice Your Skills

Write the word or phrase from the box that best completes the sentence.

Vocabulary Practice
compass rose   symbol
cardinal directions
map   legend
title

1. A _____ is a drawing of a real place.

2. A _____ stands for something real.

3. The _____ explains what the map's symbols mean.

4. The _____ helps you find directions on a map.

5. The letters N, S, E, and W stand for _____.

Map Skills Practice

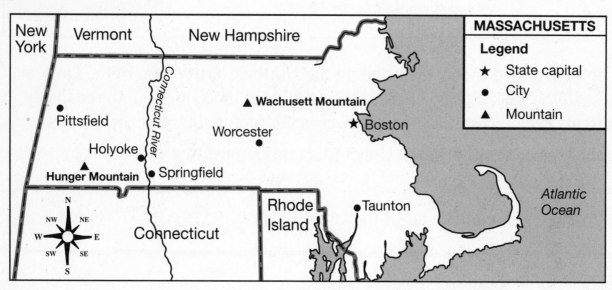

Find each place described below on the map. Write its name in the space provided.

6. A mountain west of Holyoke _____

7. A city south of Wachusett Mountain _____

8. A city along the eastern side of the Connecticut River _____

9. A city along the western side of the Connecticut River _____

Name _____ Date _____

My Neighborhood

In the space provided, draw a map of your neighborhood that is similar to the map on page 14. Your map should include at least five streets and three locations. Remember to include a title, compass rose, and legend for your map.

My Neighborhood
Maps: Read, Understand, Apply 3–4, SV9781419099427

Intermediate Directions

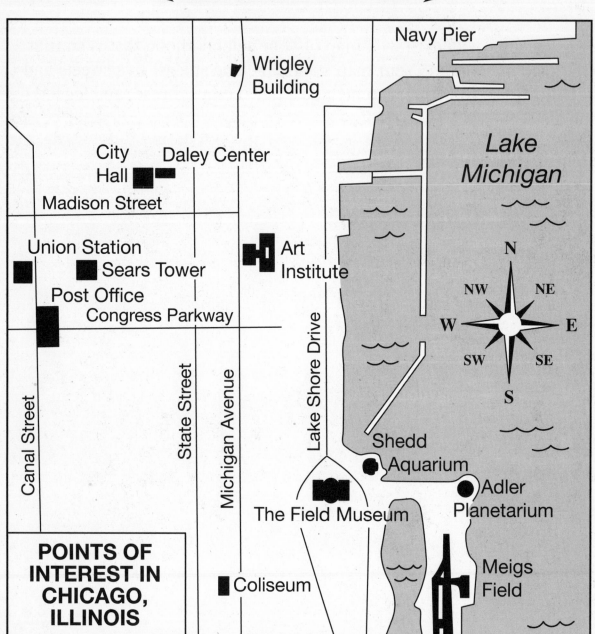

You already know about the cardinal directions—north, south, east, and west. We use the cardinal directions to find places on Earth.

Look at the map above. Suppose you are at The Field Museum in Chicago. Find it on the map. To get to the Adler Planetarium, you go east.

You decide to walk from The Field Museum to Union Station. Find Union Station on the map. Are you walking north? Are you walking west? You are walking between north and west. That direction is called northwest.

Maps: Read, Understand, Apply 3–4, SV9781419099427

Name _____   Date _____

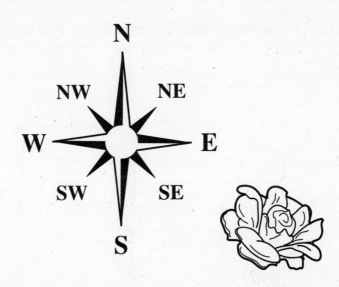

Northeast (NE), southeast (SE), southwest (SW), and northwest (NW) are **intermediate directions.** Look at the compass rose above. Find the arrows for north, east, south, and west. Then find the "in-between" arrows. These arrows point to the intermediate directions. Notice how the compass rose looks like an unfolding flower.

You can practice finding intermediate directions every time you read a compass rose. Practice now on the map on page 22.

Answer the questions.

1. From The Field Museum, which direction is each of these places?

   a. Daley Center _____

   b. Navy Pier _____

   c. Sears Tower _____

2. Find City Hall on the map. Which direction would you walk to get to each of these places?

   a. Union Station _____

   b. Art Institute _____

   c. Wrigley Building _____

Intermediate Directions
Maps: Read, Understand, Apply 3–4, SV9781419099427

Name _____ Date _____

Using Intermediate Directions on a State Map

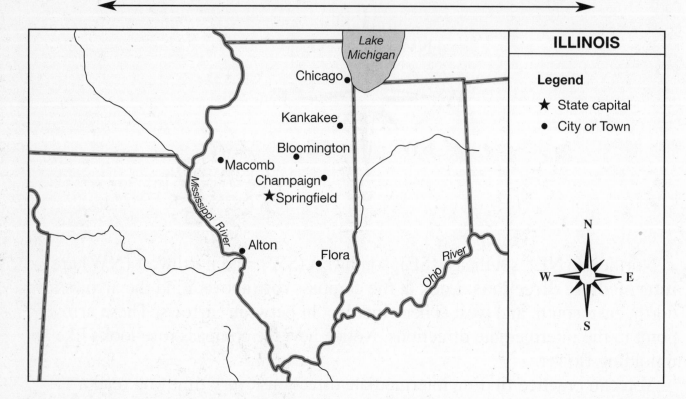

1. Read the title. This map shows _____.

2. Read the compass rose. Label the intermediate direction arrows. Use NE for northeast, SE for southeast, SW for southwest, and NW for northwest.

Write the best intermediate direction in each sentence.

3. Find Springfield, the capital of Illinois. Circle it. Draw a line from Springfield to Bloomington. Bloomington is _____ of Springfield.

4. Draw a line from Springfield to Alton. Alton is _____ of Springfield.

5. Draw a line from Springfield to Flora. Flora is _____ of Springfield.

6. Draw a line from Springfield to Macomb. Macomb is _____ of Springfield.

Name _____ Date _____

Using Intermediate Directions on a National Map

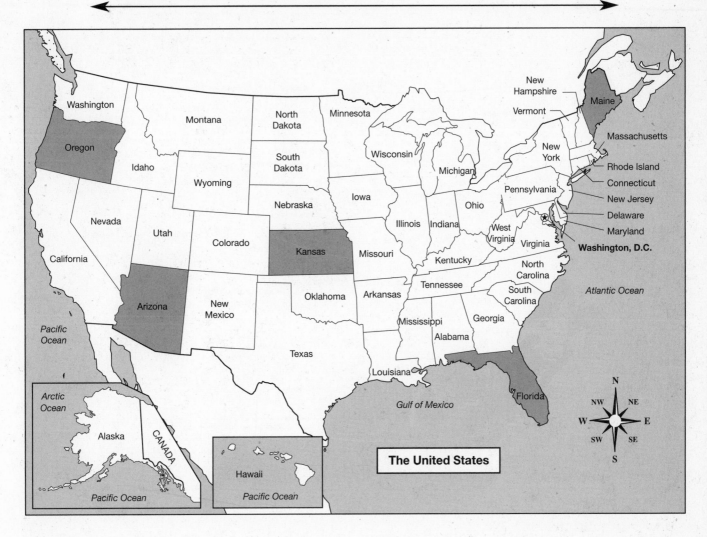

1. Which direction is between north and west? _____

2. Which direction is between south and east? _____

3. Northeast is between _____ and _____.

4. Southwest is between _____ and _____.

5. To drive from Kansas to Oregon, you go _____.

6. To drive from Kansas to Florida, you go _____.

7. To drive from Kansas to Arizona, you go _____.

8. To drive from Kansas to Maine, you go _____.

Name _____ Date _____

Using Symbols and Intermediate Directions

1. Label the intermediate directions with NE, SE, SW, and NW.

2. Find the capital of Arizona. Circle it.

Use the compass rose to find these directions.

3. Idaho is _____ of Utah.

4. Florida is in the _____ part of the United States.

5. Arizona is in the _____ part of the United States.

6. To drive from San Diego to Los Angeles, you go _____.

7. Chicago is in the _____ part of Illinois.

8. To get from Nome to Anchorage, you go _____.

Using Symbols and Intermediate Directions
Maps: Read, Understand, Apply 3–4, SV9781419099427

Directions in the Great Lakes States

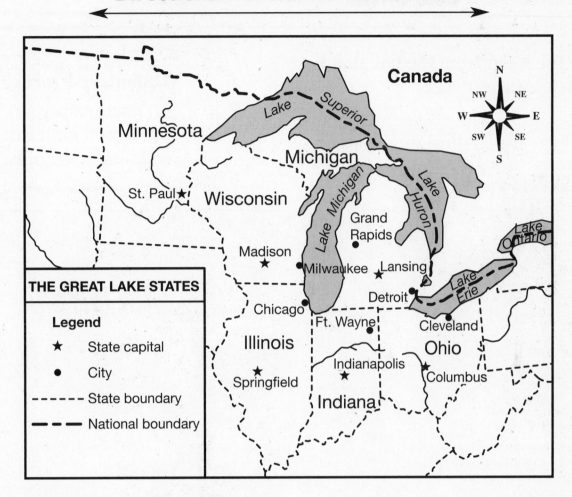

1. Trace the state boundaries in green.

2. Trace the national boundary in red.

3. Color the states yellow. Choose another light color and color Canada.

4. Find each place below on the map. Write the direction you would travel from the first place to the second place. Use cardinal and intermediate directions. The first one has been done for you.

a. Indianapolis to Columbus ___E___   **e.** Springfield to Madison _____

b. St. Paul to Madison _____   **f.** Ohio to Illinois _____

c. Lansing to Springfield _____   **g.** Wisconsin to Ohio _____

d. Grand Rapids to Ft. Wayne _____   **h.** Lake Erie to Lake Superior _____

Practice Your Skills

Write the word from the box that best completes the sentence.

1. _____ directions are between the cardinal directions.

Map Skills Practice

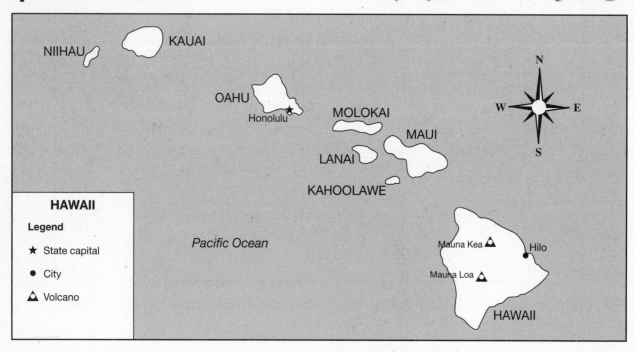

2. Finish the compass rose on the map above. Add the intermediate directions NE, SE, SW, and NW.

3. Find the island of Lanai on the map. Circle it.

4. Draw a line from Lanai to Maui. Maui is _____ of Lanai.

5. Draw a line from Lanai to the big island of Hawaii. Hawaii is _____ of Lanai.

6. Draw a line from Lanai to Oahu. Oahu is _____ of Lanai.

7. Find the city of Hilo on the big island of Hawaii.

   a. Which volcano is southwest of Hilo? _____

   b. Which volcano is northwest of Hilo? _____

Name _____ Date _____

My Route to School

Think about the route you travel from home to school every day. Write the route on the lines. Be sure to list the streets on the route as well as the direction you travel on each street. Use cardinal and intermediate directions.

_____

_____

_____

_____

Now that you have written your route, draw a map of the streets used on your route. Use the space below for your map. Your map should include a title, compass rose, and legend.

My Route to School
Maps: Read, Understand, Apply 3–4, SV9781419099427

Geography Theme: Place

Place describes a location that has physical and human features. These features make it special. Physical features include things that are found naturally, such as bodies of water and plants. Human features are made by people. They include parks, buildings, bridges, and railroads.

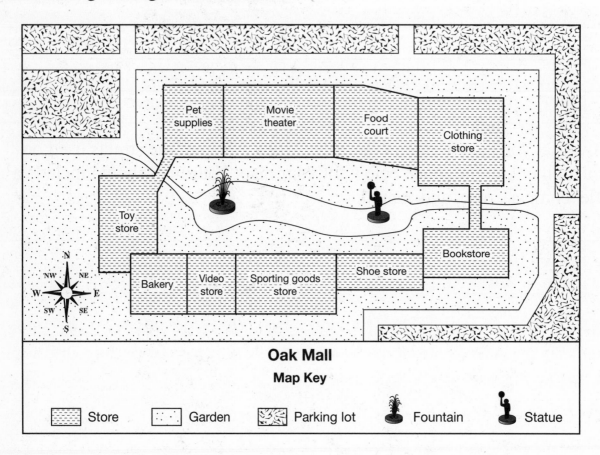

Oak Mall

Map Key

[ ] Store   [ ] Garden   [ ] Parking lot   🌿 Fountain   👤 Statue

1. What store is north of the bookstore?

_____

2. List three features of Oak Mall.

_____

_____

3. Find the toy store on the map. Circle it. Mark **P** on it if it is a physical feature. Mark **H** if it is a human feature.

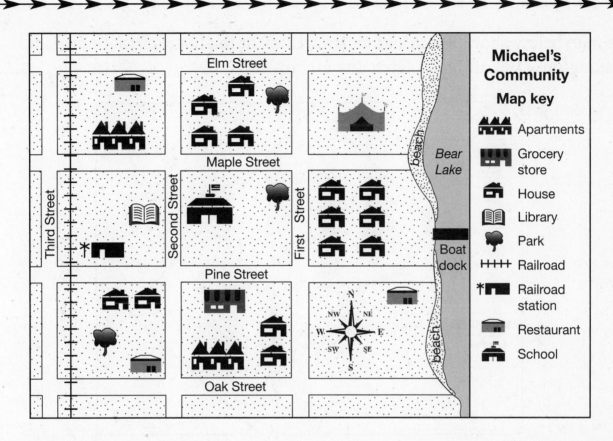

1. Find the fairgrounds on the map above. They are west of Bear Lake. Label them on the map. Write **P** on the map if they are a physical feature. Write **H** on the map if they are a human feature.

2. Name a physical feature of Michael's community. Label it with **P** on the map.

_____

3. What features in Michael's community make it different from your community?

_____

_____

_____

Name _____ Date _____

The map below shows Washington, D.C. Look at the features that make Washington, D.C., different from any other place.

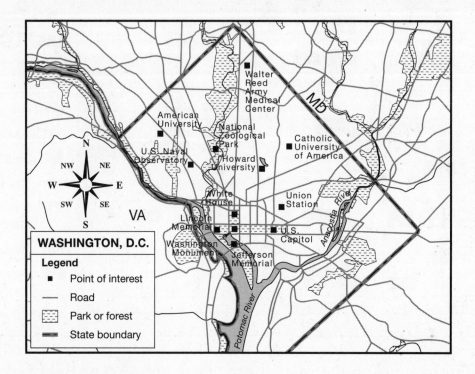

1. One human feature of Washington, D.C., is Rock Creek Park. This park is north of the National Zoological Park. Use the symbol for park in the legend and label Rock Creek Park on the map.

2. Name a physical feature of Washington, D.C., shown on the map.

_____

3. Find the U.S. Capitol on the map. It is southeast of the White House. Circle the U.S. Capitol. Write **P** next to it if it is a physical feature; write **H** if it is a human feature.

4. What are two other human features of Washington, D.C., shown on the map?

_____

_____

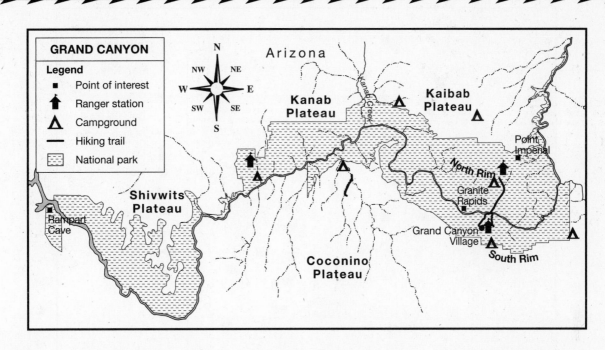

1. Label the Colorado River on the map. Write **P** next to it if it is a physical feature; write **H** if it is a human feature.

2. What are two other physical features of the Grand Canyon?

_____

3. The Grand Canyon Village is a human feature of the Grand Canyon. It is in the southeastern part of the Grand Canyon. Circle the Grand Canyon Village.

4. What are two other human features of the Grand Canyon?

_____

5. Describe how the features of the Grand Canyon differ from the features of Washington, D.C.

_____

_____

_____

_____

Name _____ Date _____

Resource Maps

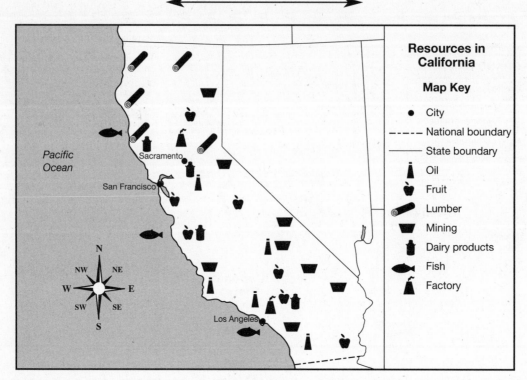

This map shows the resources in California. **Resources** are things people can use. The map also shows the areas where those resources are found. Find the factory symbols on the map. A **factory** is a place where resources are made into other things.

1. Read the title. The title tells you the purpose of the map and what the map shows. What is the title?

   _____

2. Study the key. Read the meanings of the symbols. Find each symbol on the map. Which resources are near cities?

   _____

3. Read the compass rose. Find north on the map. Which resources are in the north?

   _____

   Which resources are in the south?_____

Maps: Read, Understand, Apply 3–4, SV9781419099427

Name _____   Date _____

The resources you see on the map on page 34 can be grouped in different ways. Grouping them makes them easier to study and remember. Some of the resources come from animals. Some come from plants. Others are minerals found in the earth. This table shows California's resources listed in the three groups.

California's Resources		
Animal Resources	Plant Resources	Mineral Resources
dairy products	fruit	mining
fish	lumber	oil

Resources can also be grouped by place. Which symbols are mainly in the north? in the south? in the east? in the west? This table shows California's resources by place.

California's Resources by Place	
Resources mainly in the east:	mining fruit
Resources mainly in the west:	fishing dairy products
Resources mainly in the north:	lumber
Resources mainly in the south:	oil

Name _____ Date _____

Reading a Resource Map

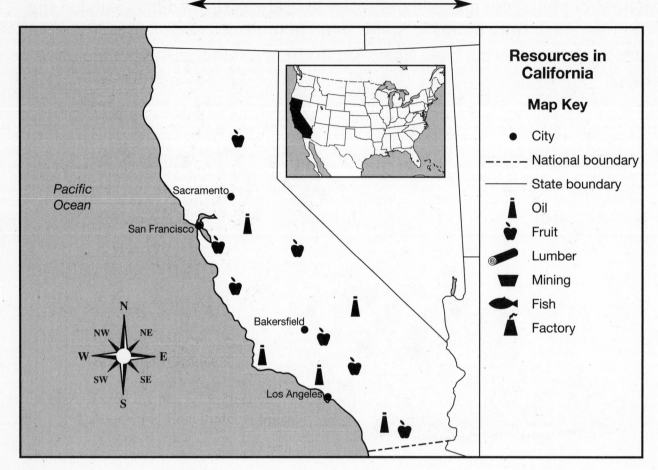

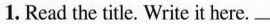

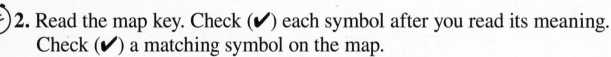

1. Read the title. Write it here. _____

2. Read the map key. Check (✔) each symbol after you read its meaning. Check (✔) a matching symbol on the map.

3. Read the compass rose. Circle the north arrow.

4. Draw four factory symbols, one each near San Francisco, Los Angeles, Bakersfield, and Sacramento.

5. Draw three mining symbols along California's eastern boundary.

6. Draw three fishing symbols off the western coastline.

7. Draw three lumber symbols near the northern boundary.

Maps: Read, Understand, Apply 3–4, SV9781419099427

Name _____ Date _____

Resources and Products in Texas

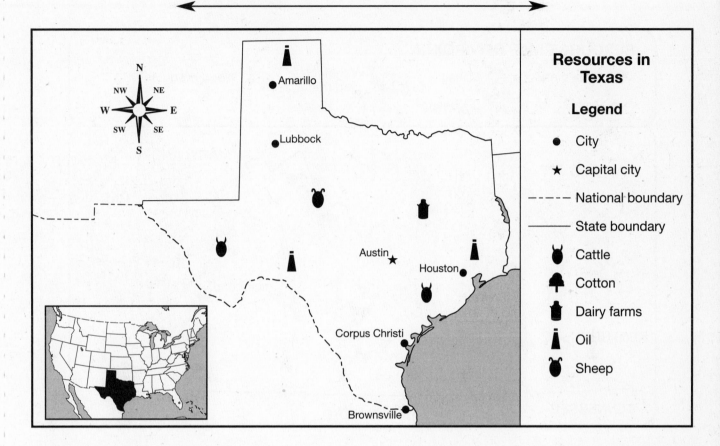

1. The title of the map is _____.

2. The state capital is _____.

3. Draw a cotton symbol southwest of Corpus Christi.

4. Draw one cotton symbol north of Austin, one north of Lubbock, and one north of Brownsville.

5. Draw two oil symbols, one near Lubbock and one near Houston.

6. Draw two cattle symbols, one northwest of Amarillo and one northwest of Austin.

7. Circle the resource that is produced in more places.

   a. cotton or dairy   **b.** sheep or cattle   **c.** oil or cotton

Maps: Read, Understand, Apply 3–4, SV9781419099427

Name _____   Date _____

Resources and Products in Virginia

←—————————————————→

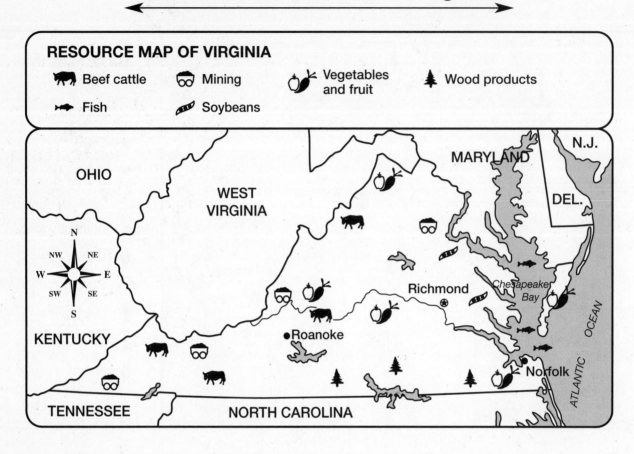

RESOURCE MAP OF VIRGINIA

- Beef cattle
- Fish
- Mining
- Soybeans
- Vegetables and fruit
- Wood products

1. What is the title of this map? _____

2. Beef cattle are mainly found in the _____ part of Virginia.

3. The two main resources in the southwestern tip of Virginia are

_____.

4. The main product in the Chesapeake Bay area of Virginia is

_____.

5. The product found north and east of Richmond is

_____.

Resources and Products in Virginia
Maps: Read, Understand, Apply 3–4, SV9781419099427

Name _____ Date _____

Using a Resource Map

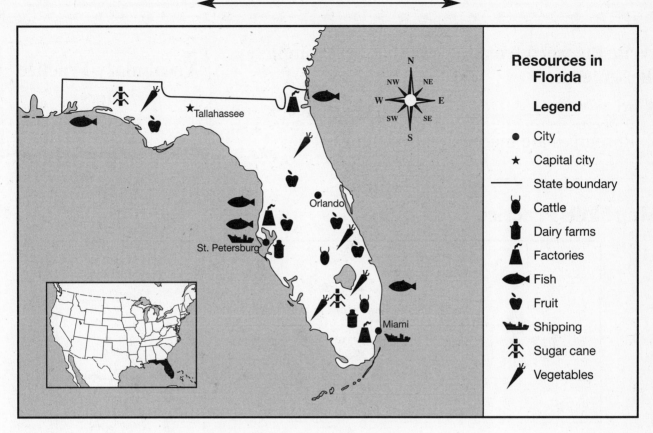

1. What does the map show? (What is the title?)

_____

2. Circle Florida on the small U.S. map. Is Florida in the northern or southern part of the United States? _____

3. In which direction do you travel to go from St. Petersburg to Orlando?

_____

4. In which direction do you travel to go from St. Petersburg to Miami?

_____

5. Which cities are on the coast?

_____

6. Name three of the most important resources in Florida.

_____

Name _____ Date _____

Practice Your Skills

Write the word from the box that best completes the sentence.

1. A _____ is something that people use.

2. Resources are made into other things at a

_____.

Map Skills Practice

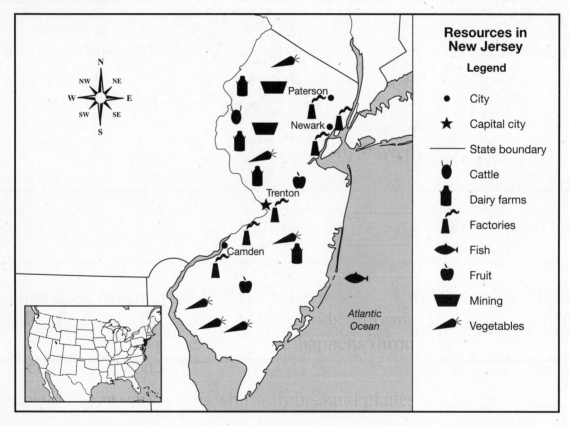

3. Cattle and dairy farms are mainly in the _____ part of New Jersey.

4. The main resource in the south is _____.

5. Circle the resource that is produced in more places.

   a. cattle or dairy   **b.** fruit or fish   **c.** mining or vegetables

6. What resources are located near the cities? _____

Name _____ Date _____

Resources in My State

In the space below, create a resource map of your state. Use an almanac or an encyclopedia to determine what resources are available in your state. Your map should include a title, compass rose, legend, and a symbol for each resource.

Maps: Read, Understand, Apply 3–4, SV9781419099427

Name _____ Date _____

Landform Maps

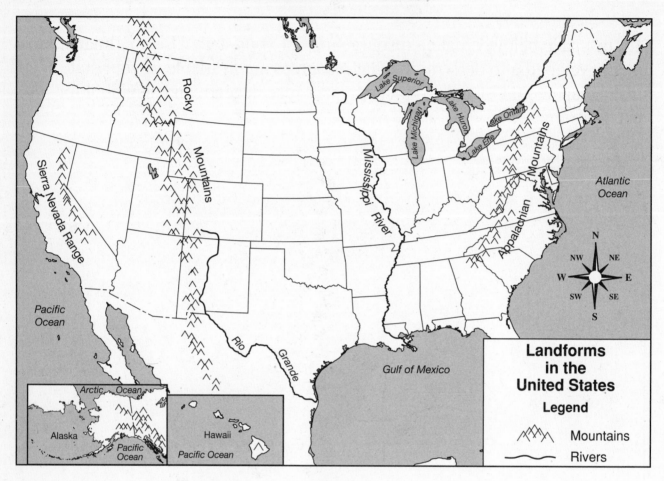

Map A

The shape of the land can be shown on maps in many different ways. A **landform map** shows the shape of the land.

The landform map on this page shows mountains. Find the symbol for mountains in the legend. This map also shows rivers, large lakes, and oceans.

The landform map on the next page shows areas of landforms. The areas are different shadings. The highest landforms are the darkest shade. The lowest landforms are the lightest shade. These are **plains,** or flatlands.

Find the areas of plateaus. A **plateau** is high, flat land.

Find the Gulf of Mexico. A **gulf** is a large body of water that cuts deep into the land.

Land next to the ocean is called the **coast**. Look for the states that have a coast.

Name _____ Date _____

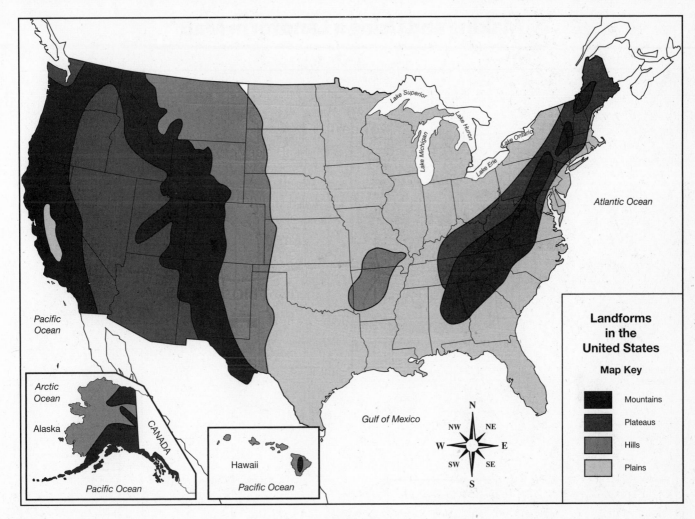

Map B

Compare Map A and Map B.

1. What landforms are only on Map B? _____

_____

2. What bodies of water are only on Map A? _____

_____

3. Are there more mountains in the eastern or the western United States?

_____

4. Where are most of the plains? _____

5. What landform is on the West Coast? _____

6. Circle the label for a gulf on both maps.

Landform Maps
Maps: Read, Understand, Apply 3–4, SV9781419099427

Name _____ Date _____

Making and Using a Landform Map

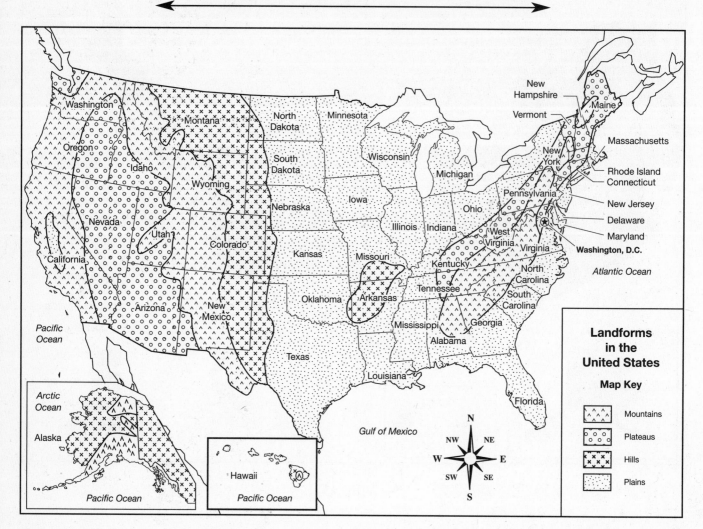

 1. Read the title. Write it here. _____

2. Read the compass rose. Circle the intermediate direction arrows.

3. Color the map key. Use colored pens or pencils. Choose four colors for the landform areas.

4. Color the map to match the key.

5. Which landform(s) does your state have?

_____

_____

Name _____ Date _____

Reading a Landform Map

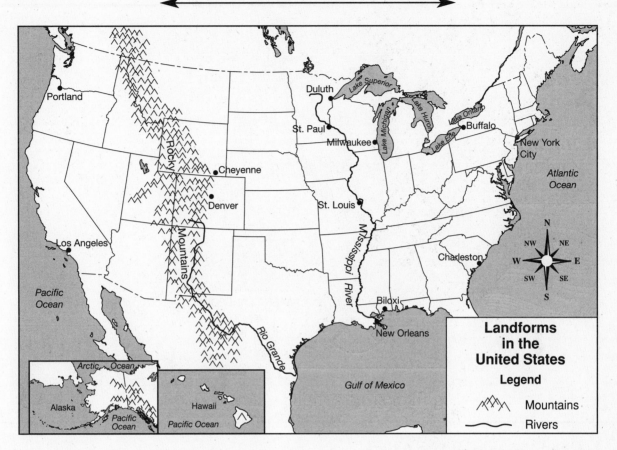

1. The title of the map is _____.

2. Read the compass rose. Circle the east arrow.

3. Name a city on the West Coast. _____

4. Name a city on the East Coast. _____

5. Name a city on the Gulf of Mexico coast. _____

6. Name two cities on the edge of the Great Lakes.

_____

7. Name two cities on the eastern edge of the Rocky Mountains.

_____

8. Name two cities on the Mississippi River.

_____

Name _____   Date _____

Landforms in Alaska

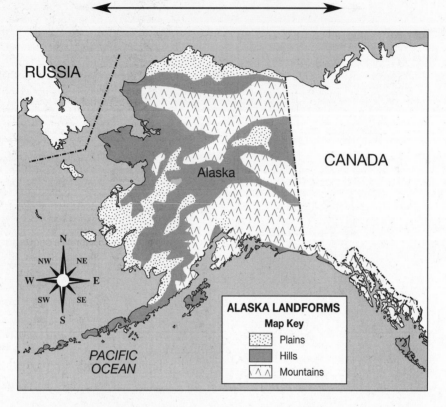

1. Read the title. Write it here.

   _____

2. Read the compass rose. Circle the south arrow.

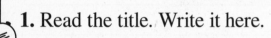

3. What kind of landform occupies the least amount of space in Alaska?

   _____

4. What kind of landform is mostly found in the southeast part of Alaska?

   _____

5. What kind of landform is found along the northern coast?

   _____

6. Are there more hills or plains in Alaska? _____

Maps: Read, Understand, Apply 3–4, SV9781419099427

Name _____ Date _____

Landforms in New York

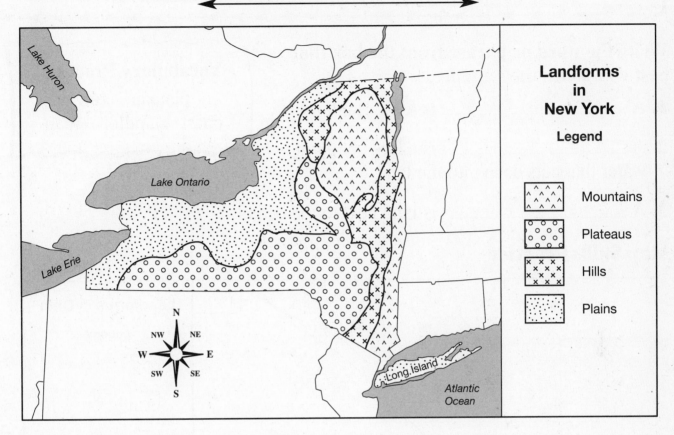

1. Color the legend. Use colored pencils or pens. Choose four colors for the landform areas.

2. Color the map to match the key.

3. New York's plains are mostly in the _____.

4. New York's mountains are mostly in the _____.

5. What lakes form part of New York's western boundary?

_____

6. What landforms are on Long Island? _____

7. What landforms border large lakes? _____

Maps: Read, Understand, Apply 3–4, SV9781419099427

Name _____ Date _____

Practice Your Skills

Write the word or phrase from the box that best completes the sentence.

Vocabulary Practice
plateau   gulf
coast   landform map

1. A _____ is high, flat land.

2. A _____ is a large body of water that cuts deep into the land.

3. A _____ is land next to the ocean.

Map Skills Practice

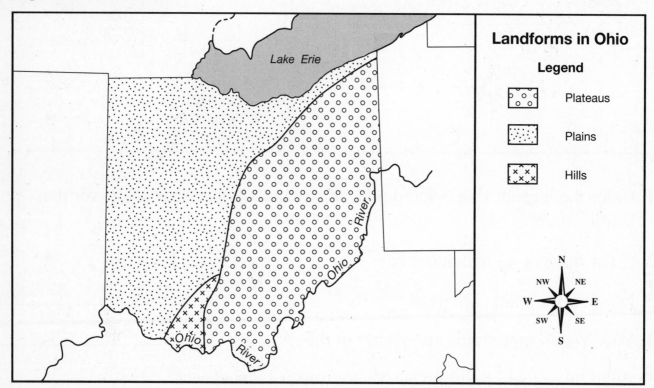

Landforms in Ohio

Legend

Plateaus

Plains

Hills

4. Color the landform areas and legend symbols to match.

5. Ohio's plains are mostly in which direction? _____

6. Ohio's plateaus are mostly in the _____.

7. What lake forms part of Ohio's northern boundary? _____

8. What river forms Ohio's southern boundary? _____

How Landforms Affect What I Do

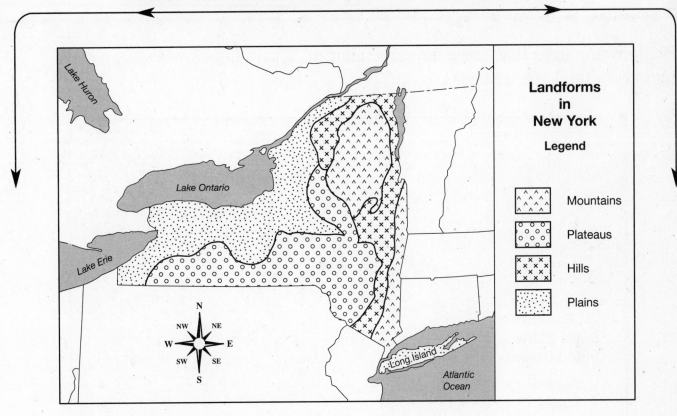

Identify the areas of New York where the following activities would most likely take place. Label the areas of the map with the name of the activity.

farming   hiking

downhill skiing   camping

swimming   fishing

mining

Pick three activities above and describe how landforms might affect each.

_____

_____

_____

Name _____   Date _____

Geography Theme: Regions

Regions are areas that share the same feature. The map below shows plant regions in the United States.

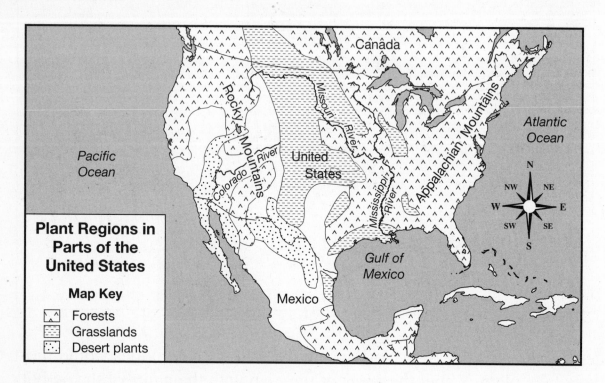

1. What three plant regions are shown on this map?

_____

2. Which plant region is largest?

_____

3. Find the Missouri River on the map. Circle it. What kinds of plants mostly grow along the Missouri River?

_____

4. What kinds of plants grow along the border of the United States and Mexico?

_____

Name _____ Date _____

The map shows Diamond Park—one of 12 community parks in Park City. All the parks in Park City have the same features.

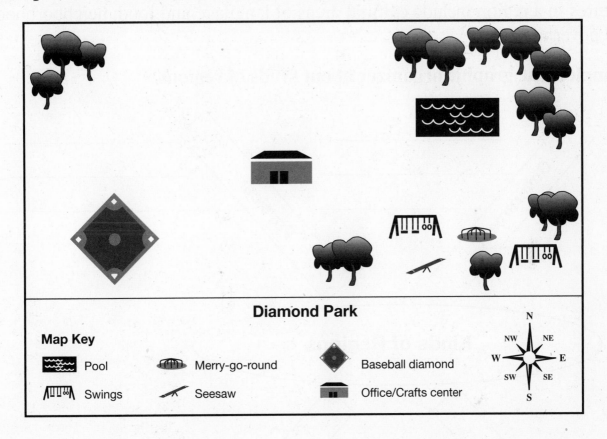

Diamond Park

Map Key

Pool   Merry-go-round   Baseball diamond

Swings   Seesaw   Office/Crafts center

1. There are tennis courts north of the baseball diamond. Write **TC** on the map for the tennis courts.

2. What direction is the baseball diamond from the pool?

_____

3. What activity is held in the Diamond Park office building?

_____

4. Why do you think the parks in Park City form a region?

_____

Name _____ Date _____

Areas in a region can share physical or human features. Regions can be described by the physical features of climate, plant life, or landforms. Human features in a region include cultural areas of language and food, neighborhoods, and government.

Complete the graphic organizer about kinds of regions.

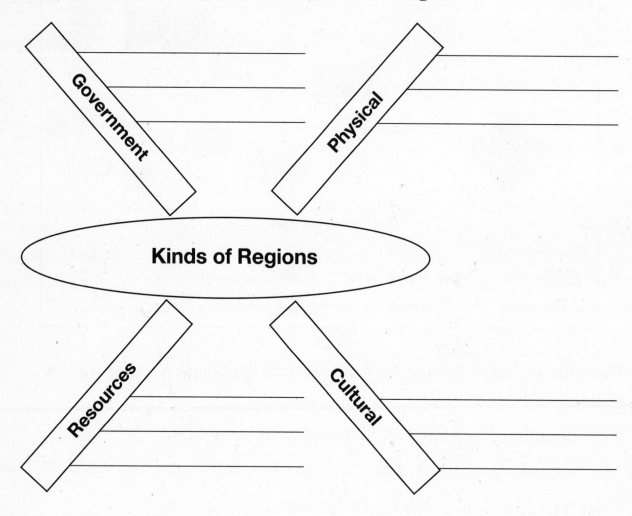

Name _____ Date _____

Landforms are one way that places are grouped into regions. People living in each region use the resources of the place to live. Animals are like people in that they use what is in their environment to survive.

Read each sentence about an animal. Write the name of the animal in the correct column in the table below to show where it lives.

1. The goats here can leap from one rocky cliff to another.

2. The kind of fox here has big ears that help it lose its body heat in high temperatures.

3. The buffalo grazes here for its food.

4. A lizard lies under the sand here to escape the sun's rays.

5. The harvest mouse builds its nest here in the stems of tall grasses.

6. The lion here is a good climber and has a warm coat for snowy areas.

7. The kangaroo rat here gets its only water from the seeds it eats.

8. The bighorn sheep here finds food at very high altitudes.

9. The pronghorn sometimes meets its enemies at waterholes here, but it can escape them by running very fast.

Mountains	Deserts	Plains

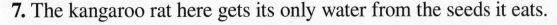

Geography Theme: Regions
Maps: Read, Understand, Apply 3–4, SV9781419099427

Name _____ Date _____

Map Grids

⟷

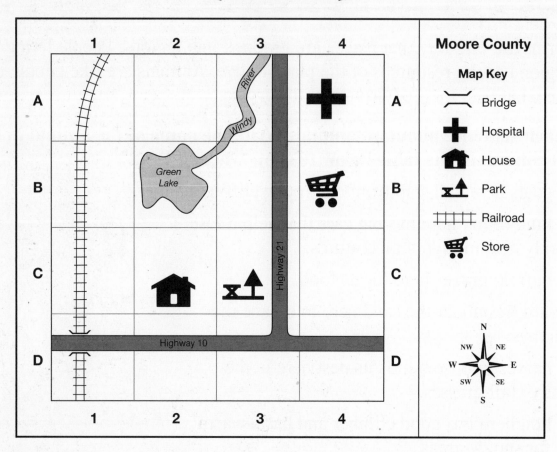

Moore County

Map Key

⌣ Bridge

✚ Hospital

🏠 House

⬆ Park

▦ Railroad

🛒 Store

Sometimes you want to say exactly where a place is on a map. You can do this by using a grid. A **grid** is a pattern of lines that cross each other. The lines form squares.

1. Each row of squares has a letter. Find the letters at each side of the map.

What letters are used? _____

2. Each column of squares has a number. Find the numbers across the top and

the bottom of the map. What numbers are used? _____

Each square on the map is named with a letter and a number.
Here is how to find square A-2. Put your finger on the letter A. Move your finger across the row. Stop when you come to column 2. This is square A-2.

3. Can you find square C-3? Circle it.

4. In which square is the store? _____

5. Which squares does the railroad go through? _____

Maps: Read, Understand, Apply 3–4, SV9781419099427

Name _____   Date _____

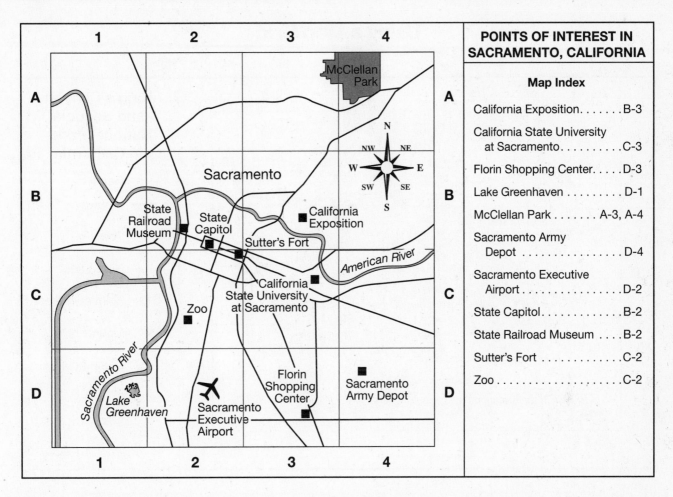

POINTS OF INTEREST IN SACRAMENTO, CALIFORNIA

Map Index

California Exposition. B-3

California State University
   at Sacramento. C-3

Florin Shopping Center. D-3

Lake Greenhaven D-1

McClellan Park A-3, A-4

Sacramento Army
   Depot D-4

Sacramento Executive
   Airport D-2

State Capitol. B-2

State Railroad Museum B-2

Sutter's Fort C-2

Zoo C-2

You can find a place on a map grid by looking it up in the map index. A **map index** is an alphabetical list of the places on the map. A map index lists each place with the letter and number of its grid square.

Look at the map on this page. It shows places of interest in Sacramento, California. To find places on the map, you use the map index. Suppose you want to visit the zoo. Look up "zoo" in the map index. The map index tells you that the zoo is in square C-2. To find this square on the map, put your finger on the C and slide it across row C until you reach column 2. This is square C-2. You can now find the zoo.

1. Use the map index to find Lake Greenhaven. In which grid square is it

   located? _____

2. Look up Florin Shopping Center in the map index. In which grid square

   is it located? _____

Map Grids
Maps: Read, Understand, Apply 3–4, SV9781419099427

Name _____ Date _____

Using a Map Grid

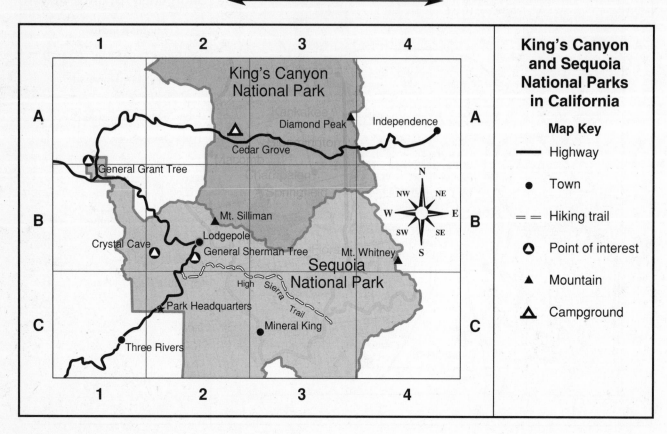

King's Canyon and Sequoia National Parks in California

Map Key
— Highway
● Town
== Hiking trail
⬢ Point of interest
▲ Mountain
△ Campground

1. The following places are in which grid squares?

   a. Independence _____   **d.** Mt. Silliman _____

   b. Park Headquarters _____   **e.** Cedar Grove _____

   c. Mineral King _____   **f.** Mt. Whitney _____

2. High Sierra Trail goes through which squares? _____

3. Find each location. Use the compass rose to find the direction. The first one has been done for you.

   a. from Lodgepole to Diamond Peak   _____NE_____

   b. from General Sherman Tree to General Grant Tree _____

   c. from Independence to Cedar Grove   _____

   d. from Crystal Cave to Park Headquarters   _____

Name _____ Date _____

Making a Map Grid

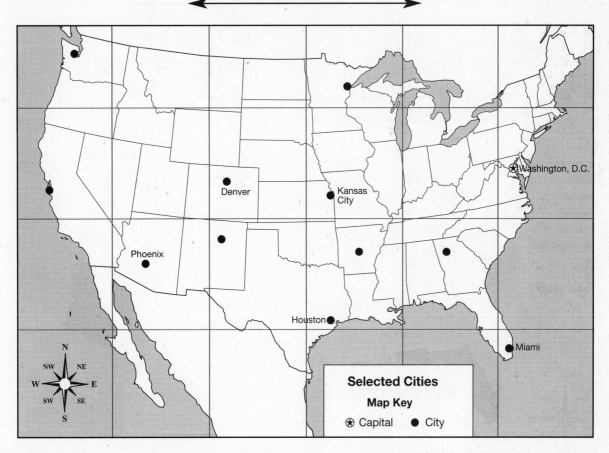

Selected Cities

Map Key

⊛ Capital   ● City

1. Finish the grid. Write the letters A, B, C, and D down each side. Write the numbers 1, 2, 3, 4, 5, and 6 across the top and bottom.

2. In which square is each place?

a. Washington, D.C. _____   **d.** Miami _____

b. Houston _____   **e.** Phoenix _____

c. Denver _____   **f.** Kansas City _____

3. Find these cities on the map. Label each city.

San Francisco   B-1   Olympia   A-1   Little Rock   C-4

Duluth   A-4   Santa Fe C-3   Atlanta   C-5

4. If you drove from Denver to Washington, D.C., what squares would you

drive in? _____

Making a Map Grid

Maps: Read, Understand, Apply 3–4, SV9781419099427

Name _____   Date _____

Finding Places on a State Map

←————————————————————————————→

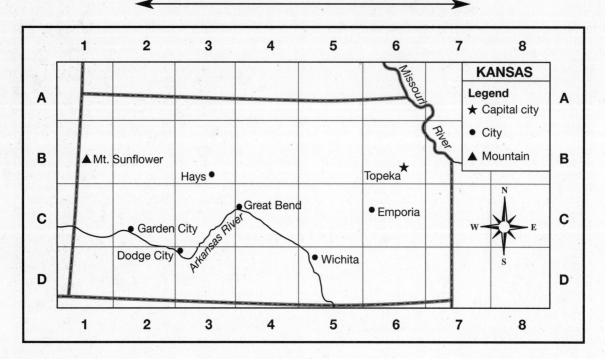

1. Read the title. This map's title is _____.

2. Read the compass rose. Label the intermediate direction arrows.

3. Read the grid. There are _____ rows and _____ columns on the grid.

4. The capital city of Kansas is in square B-6. What is the name of this city?

_____

5. The highest point in Kansas is in square B-1. What is the name of this mountain? _____

6. The largest city in Kansas is in square D-5. What is the name of this city?

_____

7. Garden City is a city in square C-2. Locate it on your map. This city is on which river? _____

8. Name two other cities on the Arkansas River. Then write the letter and number of their grid squares.

_____

►►

Name _____ Date _____

Finding Places on a Regional Map

←→

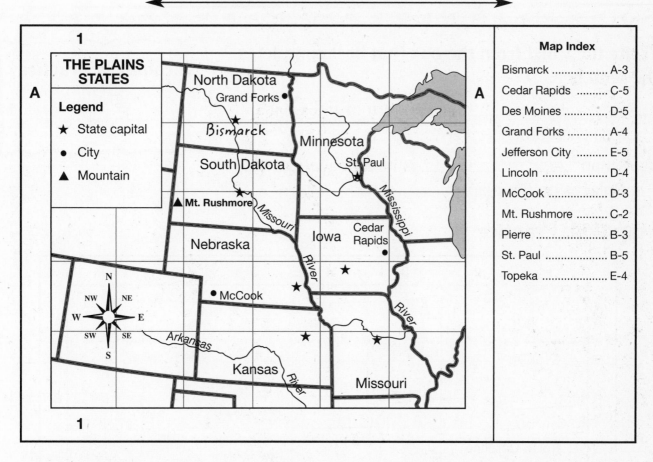

Map Index

Bismarck A-3
Cedar Rapids C-5
Des Moines D-5
Grand Forks A-4
Jefferson City E-5
Lincoln D-4
McCook D-3
Mt. Rushmore C-2
Pierre B-3
St. Paul B-5
Topeka E-4

1. Finish the map grid. Write the letters B, C, D, and E down each side of the map. Write the numbers 2, 3, 4, 5, and 6 across the top and bottom of the map. The first letter and number are done for you.

2. Use the index to find the places listed below. Circle each one on the map. Then write the name of the state where each place is located.

a. Mt. Rushmore _____   **c.** Cedar Rapids _____

b. McCook _____   **d.** Grand Forks _____

3. Use the index to locate each state capital listed below. Write the name of each state capital where it belongs on the map. Then write the name of the state where each capital is located. The first one has been done for you.

a. Bismarck   *North Dakota*   **d.** Des Moines _____

b. Jefferson City _____   **e.** Lincoln _____

c. Pierre _____   **f.** Topeka _____

Practice Your Skills

Write the word from the box that best completes the sentence.

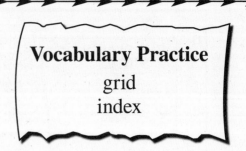

Vocabulary Practice
grid
index

1. A _____ is a pattern of lines that cross each other.

2. A map _____ is an alphabetical list of places on the map.

Map Skills Practice

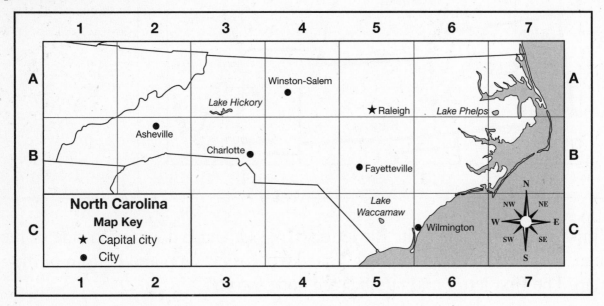

3. Name North Carolina's capital and the letter and number of its grid square.

_____

4. Complete the map index below.

a. _____	B-2	**e.** Lake Phelps	_____
b. Charlotte	_____	**f.** Lake Waccamaw	_____
c. Fayetteville	_____	**g.** Wilmington	_____
d. _____	A-3	**h.** _____	A-4

My Treasure Map

In the space below, create a treasure map that might lead your friends to a buried treasure. Your setting might be your school, your house, or your neighborhood. Your map should include a grid to aid your friends in their search. Be sure to include a title, compass rose, legend, and map index.

Maps: Read, Understand, Apply 3–4, SV9781419099427

Name _____ Date _____

Distance and Scale

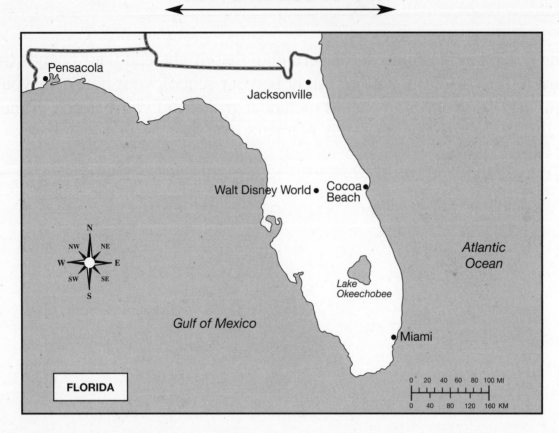

A map is more than a photograph. A photograph cannot show all the places that a map can. A map helps us locate places. It also helps us figure distances between places. **Distance** is how far apart places are.

Florida is 450 miles long. A map cannot be that long! We must make maps small enough to hold. So on this map of Florida, one inch equals one hundred miles.

How do we know that? We find out that one inch equals one hundred miles by reading the **map scale**. A map scale looks like this:

The marks and numbers along the top stand for distance in miles. The marks and numbers along the bottom stand for distance in kilometers. **Miles** and **kilometers** are two ways of measuring distance.

Find the map scale on the map above.

1. What letters stand for <u>miles</u>? _____

2. What letters stand for <u>kilometers</u>? _____

Maps: Read, Understand, Apply 3–4, SV9781419099427

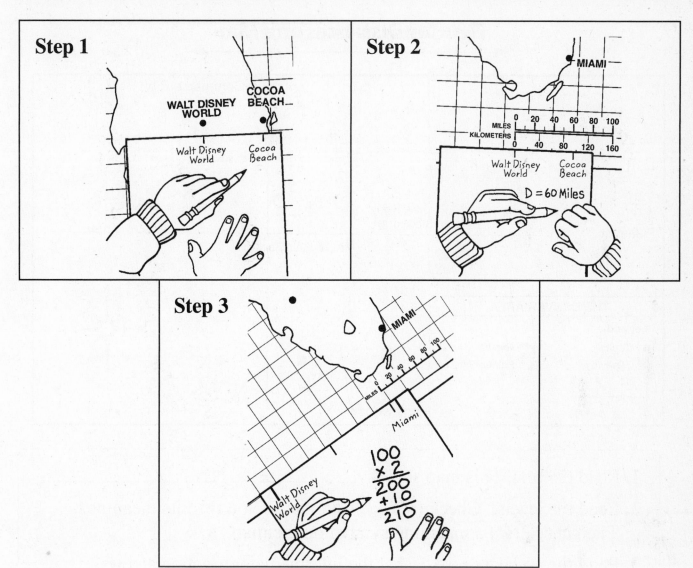

You are on vacation in Florida. You want to find the distance between Walt Disney World and two cities in Florida. Here's how you use the map scale.

Step 1: Place the edge of a sheet of paper in a straight line from Walt Disney World to Cocoa Beach. Mark your paper below each city.

Step 2: Lay the edge of your paper along the scale. Your left-hand mark should be below "0." Read the scale numbers nearest your right-hand mark. The numbers tell you that Walt Disney World and Cocoa Beach are 60 miles apart.

Step 3: What if the distance is more than 100 miles? Find out how many times the scale fits between your two marks. Multiply the number of times it fits by the high number on the scale. Then add the extra amount.

Name _____ Date _____

Figuring Distances on a Map

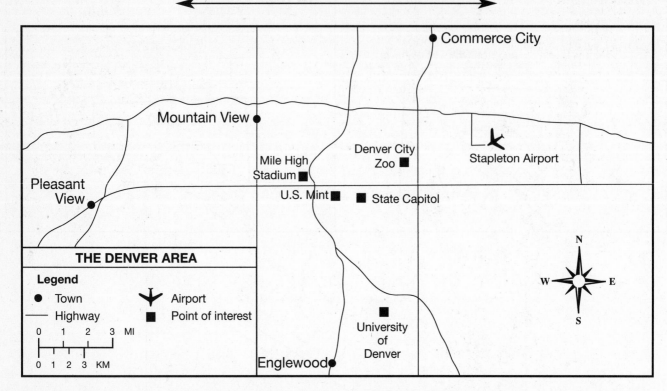

1. Read the title. This map shows _____.
2. Read the legend. Check (✔) each symbol as you read its meaning. Then check (✔) a matching symbol on the map.
3. Read the compass rose. Label the intermediate direction arrows.
4. Read the map scale. The scale goes up to _____ miles.

Use the map scale and the edge of a piece of paper to figure these distances. Write the distance in miles for questions 5 through 7. Write the distance in kilometers for question 8.

5. From the University of Denver to Mile High Stadium is about _____ miles.

6. From the Denver City Zoo to Englewood is about _____ miles.

7. From the State Capitol to the University of Denver is about _____ miles.

8. From Pleasant View to Mountain View is about _____ kilometers.

Maps: Read, Understand, Apply 3–4, SV9781419099427

Name _____ Date _____

Figuring Distances on a State Map

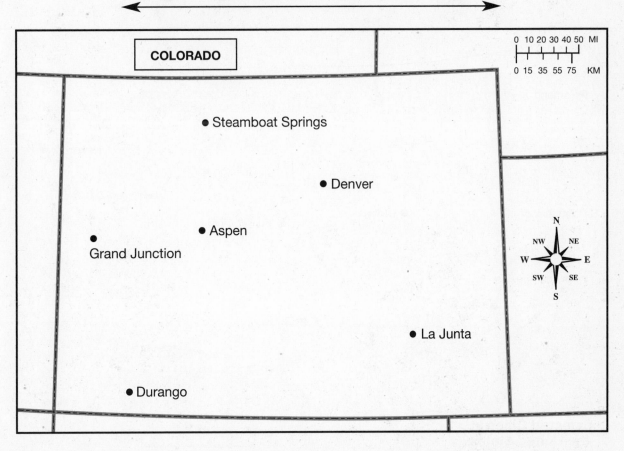

You are about to go on a flying trip through the Rocky Mountains. Your plane will land in several cities. How many miles will you travel?

Use the map scale and the edge of a sheet of paper to figure the distance.

1. Draw a line from Denver to Durango. Measure the
distance from Denver to Durango. _____ miles

2. Draw a line from Durango to Aspen. Measure the
distance from Durango to Aspen. _____ miles

3. Draw a line from Aspen to Steamboat Springs. Measure
the distance from Aspen to Steamboat Springs. _____ miles

4. Draw a line from Steamboat Springs to Denver. Measure
the distance from Steamboat Springs to Denver. _____ miles

5. How many miles did you fly? Add the number of miles
between each city. _____ miles

Name _____ Date _____

Figuring Distances on a National Map

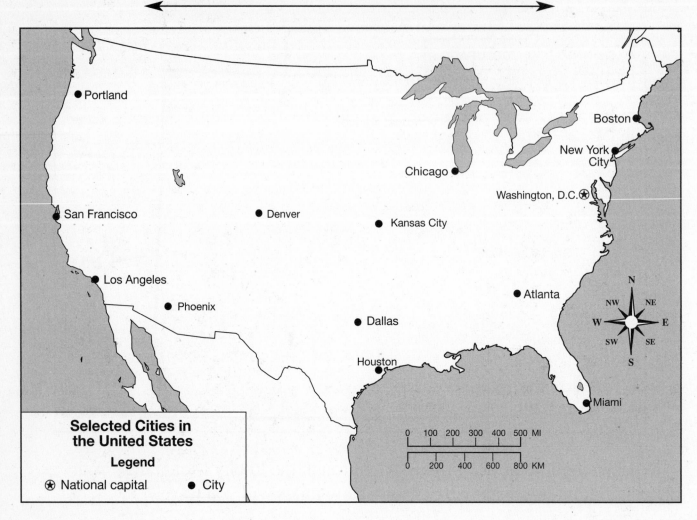

Use the map scale and the edge of a sheet of paper to find these distances.

1. From Phoenix to Dallas is about _____ miles.

2. From Portland to Chicago is about _____ miles.

3. From Boston to Kansas City is about _____ miles.

4. From Atlanta to Houston is about _____ miles.

5. From New York City to Miami is about _____ miles.

6. From Los Angeles to Chicago is about _____ miles.

7. From San Francisco to Denver is about _____ miles.

Figuring Distances on a Regional Map

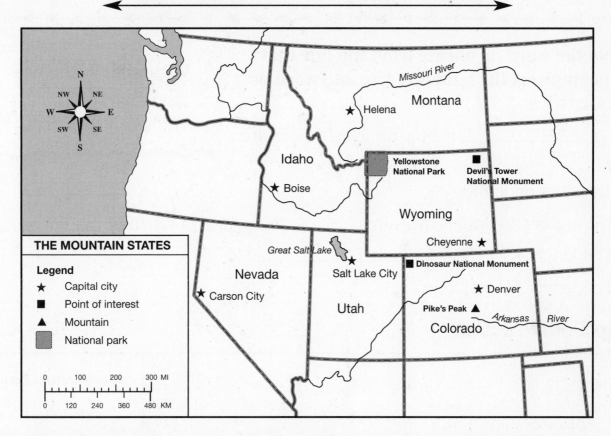

You and your family are planning a trip through the mountain states. Below is the daily log you need to complete before the trip. Finish the daily log. Use the map scale and the edge of a sheet of paper to find the distances. The first day has been done for you.

Day 1 Drive from Yellowstone National Park to Devil's Tower.

Drive ____*east*____ for about ____260____ miles.

Day 2 Drive from Devil's Tower to Dinosaur National Monument.

Drive _____ for about _____ miles.

Day 3 Drive from Dinosaur National Monument to Pike's Peak.

Drive _____ for about _____ miles.

Day 4 Drive from Pike's Peak to Cheyenne.

Drive _____ for about _____ miles.

Day 5 Drive from Cheyenne to Yellowstone National Park.

Drive _____ for about _____ miles.

Maps: Read, Understand, Apply 3–4, SV9781419099427

Name _____ Date _____

Practice Your Skills

Write the word or phrase from the box that best completes the sentence. Use one word or phrase twice.

1. _____ is how far apart places are.

2. A _____ is used to figure distances on a map.

3. Kilometers and miles measure _____ on Earth.

4. The letters KM stand for _____.

5. The letters MI stand for _____.

Map Skills Practice

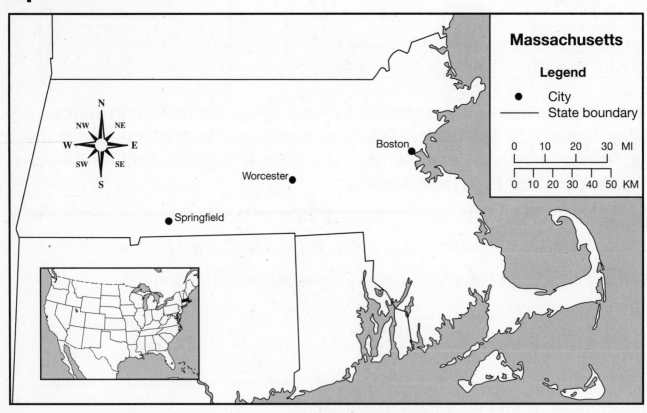

Use the scale and a sheet of paper to find these distances.

6. Springfield is about _____ miles from Worcester.

7. Boston is about _____ miles from Springfield.

Maps: Read, Understand, Apply 3–4, SV9781419099427

Name _____ Date _____

My Classroom

Work with a friend to measure your classroom. On the lines below, write down the distances between walls and between important classroom landmarks. Be sure to label each distance. Determine a scale that can be used to draw a map.

_____   _____

_____   _____

_____   _____

_____   _____

_____   _____

Work on your own to draw a map of your classroom in the space below. Your map should include symbols, a map title, compass rose, legend, and map scale.

Name _____ Date _____

✴ Geography Theme: Human/Environment Interaction

Human/Environment Interaction describes how people live in their environment. The environment has resources people can use. Where there is rich soil, people can farm. People use rivers and lakes for water, for fun, and for travel.

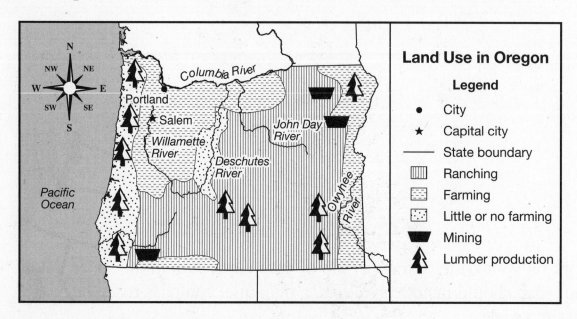

1. Where is most of the farming done in Oregon?

_____

2. In what parts of Oregon do people grow trees for lumber?

_____

3. Where is mining done in Oregon?

_____

4. Write a sentence that describes how people in Oregon live in their environment.

_____

_____

Name _____ Date _____

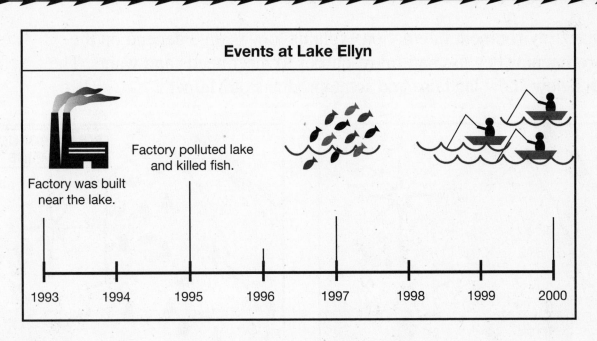

Events at Lake Ellyn

Factory was built
near the lake.

Factory polluted lake
and killed fish.

1993   1994   1995   1996   1997   1998   1999   2000

1. Name two ways Lake Ellyn changed in 1995.

_____

_____

2. Add the following events to the time line. Write each event in order on the time line.

In 2000 Lake Ellyn held a fishing derby.

In 1996 Lake Ellyn was cleaned.

In 1997 new fish were put into Lake Ellyn.

3. Look at the time line. Explain one way people changed the environment of Lake Ellyn.

_____

_____

Name _____ Date _____

Human/Environment Interaction explains how people depend on the environment. They use natural resources to meet needs and wants. The maps below show land use and some products of Maine.

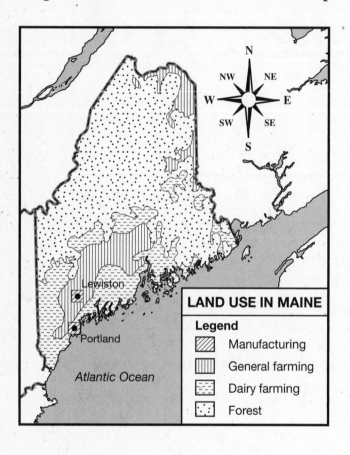

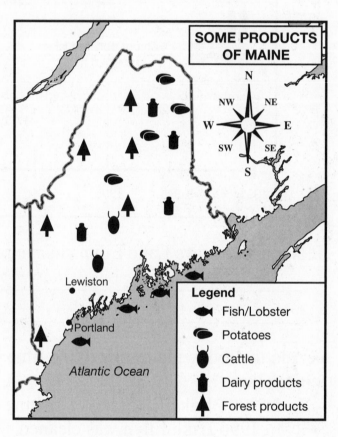

1. How do people use most of the land in southern Maine?

_____

2. What industry developed along the coast of Maine?

_____

3. Why would you expect the manufacturing of paper and wood products to be a leading industry in Maine?

_____

_____

Name _____ Date _____

Human/Environment Interaction explains how people change the environment. When people use the land and its resources to meet their needs, they change the environment. Some changes are good, but some cause problems.

1. Look at the illustration above. How have humans changed the environment? What could result from the changes?

   _____

   _____

   _____

   _____

2. How are the people in this illustration trying to change the environment?

   _____

   _____

Name _____ Date _____

Route Maps

←――――――――→

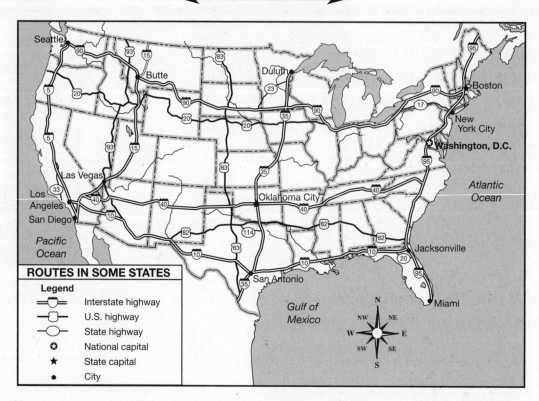

A **route** is a way of getting from one place to another. This route map shows highways in the United States. The legend shows different highway symbols used on the map. Highways are named with numbers.

Three kinds of highways are shown on this map.

Interstate highway: a main highway with many lanes. Interstate highways often cross the entire country from east to west or from north to south.

U.S. highway: a main highway that passes through more than one state.

State highway: a main road that connects cities and towns within the boundaries of one state.

Find each highway in the legend and on the map.

1. What interstate highways run north and south on the map?

_____

2. What U.S. highways can you find on the map?

_____

3. What state highways can you find on the map?

_____

Route Maps
Maps: Read, Understand, Apply 3–4, SV9781419099427

Name _____   Date _____

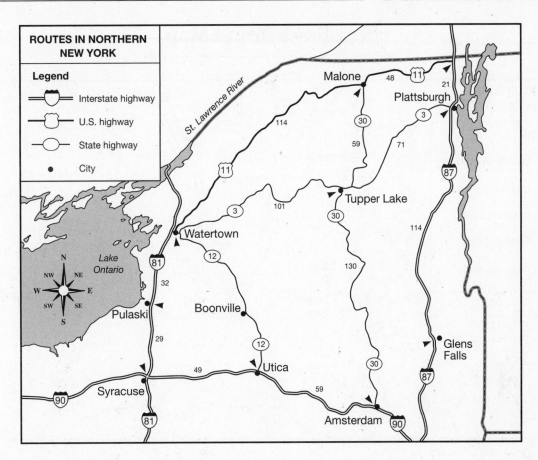

Route maps can help you find the distances between places. Look at the map above. Find the cities of Syracuse and Utica. Do you see the small triangles pointing to each city? Now find the number 49 between the triangles. This number tells you that there are 49 miles between the triangles. You now know that Syracuse and Utica are 49 miles apart.

1. How many miles apart are Utica and Amsterdam? _____ miles

2. How many miles apart are Amsterdam and Tupper Lake?

_____ miles

Sometimes you must add the numbers to find out the total distance between places. Imagine that you are driving from Pulaski to Tupper Lake. To find out how far you will drive, answer these questions.

3. How many miles is it from Pulaski to Watertown? _____ miles

4. How many miles is it from Watertown to Tupper Lake? _____ miles

5. Now add up the numbers to find the distance from Pulaski to Tupper Lake.

_____ miles

Name _____   Date _____

Reading a Route Map

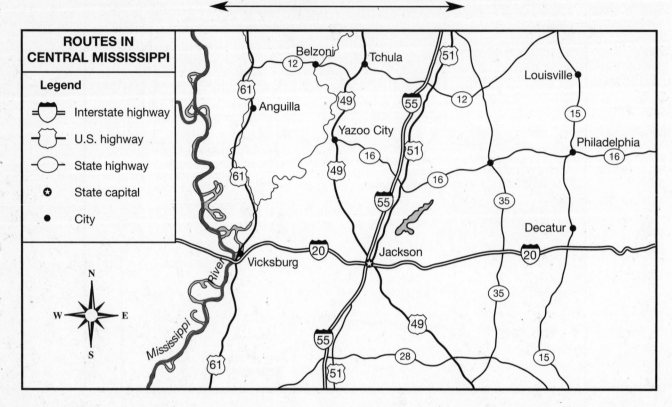

1. Read the title. This map shows _____.

2. Read the legend. The three routes shown are _____

_____.

3. Read the compass rose. Label the intermediate direction arrows.

4. What interstate highway crosses the Mississippi River? _____

5. What U.S. highway goes through Jackson? _____

6. What other cities does that route go through? _____

_____

7. Find the city where State Highways 16 and 35 meet.
   Label that city Carthage.

8. What U.S. highway goes alongside Interstate 55? _____

Name _____ Date _____

Reading a Route and Landform Map

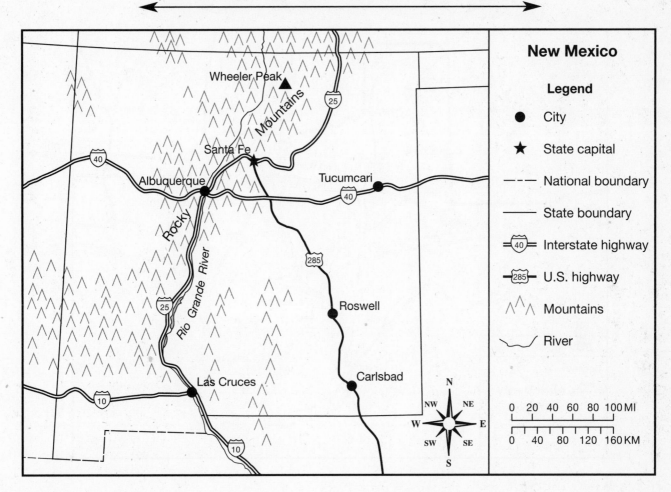

1. **What three interstate highways go through New Mexico?**

   _____

2. **Circle the city that is in the mountains.**

   Santa Fe   Roswell   Carlsbad

3. **What kind of highway is Highway 285?**

4. **To drive from Roswell to Carlsbad, which direction should you go?**

   _____ About how far is it in miles? _____ miles

5. **What two cities are on the Rio Grande River?**

   _____

Maps: Read, Understand, Apply 3–4, SV9781419099427

Name _____ Date _____

Reading Routes in Texas

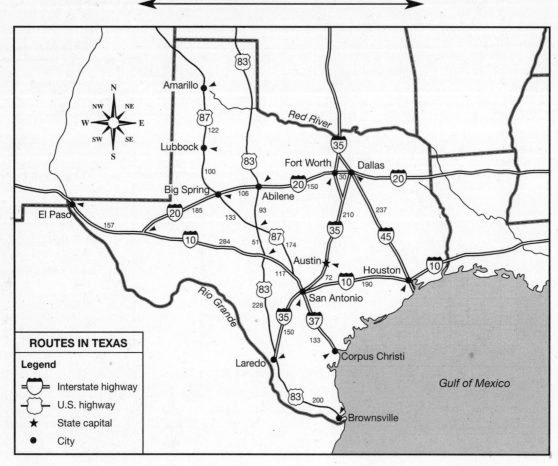

1. What does this map show? _____

2. Read the mileage numbers between the cities below. Write the distances.

   a. Austin to San Antonio _____

   b. Laredo to Brownsville _____

   c. Abilene to Fort Worth _____

   d. Dallas to Houston _____

3. Find the best route between each pair of cities below. Then add the mileage numbers to figure the distance. Write the mileage.

   a. Corpus Christi to Dallas _____

   b. El Paso to Fort Worth _____

   c. Abilene to Brownsville _____

   d. San Antonio to El Paso _____

Name _____ Date _____

Making a Route Map

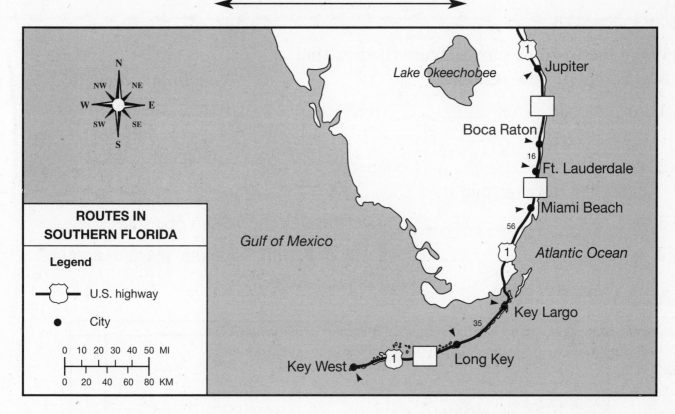

ROUTES IN SOUTHERN FLORIDA

Legend

⬡ U.S. highway

● City

0 10 20 30 40 50 MI
0 20 40 60 80 KM

Lake Okeechobee

Jupiter

Boca Raton

16

Ft. Lauderdale

Miami Beach

56

Gulf of Mexico

Atlantic Ocean

Key Largo

35

Key West

Long Key

1. Some of the mileage numbers are missing on the map above. Use the map scale to figure the distances between these towns. Choose the closest number from the box below. Then write each distance in the box on the map where it belongs.

   a. Key West to Long Key _____

   b. Jupiter to Boca Raton _____

   c. Ft. Lauderdale to Miami Beach _____

45	35
22	52
71	65

2. What is the distance between Key West and Key Largo? Use the mileage numbers from the map. _____

3. Find Jupiter on the map. Go south on U.S. Highway 1 for 139 miles. What city do you reach? _____

4. Continue south on U.S. Highway 1 to Key West. From Jupiter to Key West is _____ miles.

Maps: Read, Understand, Apply 3–4, SV9781419099427

Practice Your Skills

Write the word or phrase from the box that best completes the sentence.

Vocabulary Practice
route   state highway
U.S. highway
interstate highway

1. An _____ crosses the entire country.

2. A _____ connects cities and towns in one state.

3. A _____ passes through more than one state.

4. A _____ is a way of getting from one place to another.

Map Skills Practice

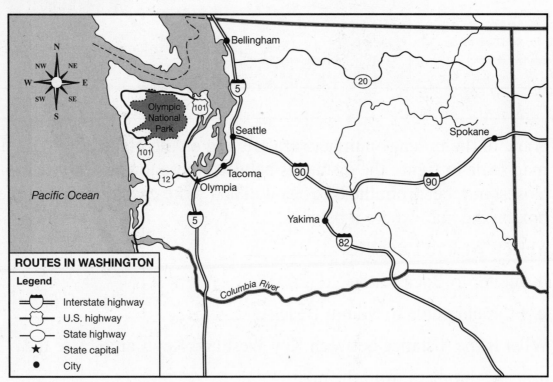

5. Find Interstate Highway 5. What cities does it pass through?

_____

6. What U.S. highway goes around Olympic National Park? _____

7. What state highway crosses the northern part of the state? _____

Name _____ Date _____

Routes in My School

Draw a route map of your school in the space below. Include routes from your classroom to the cafeteria, to the gym, and to the office. Also include the safety route your class uses during a fire drill. Your map should include a title, a legend, and a compass rose.

Maps: Read, Understand, Apply 3–4, SV9781419099427

Name _____ Date _____

Latitude

←————————→

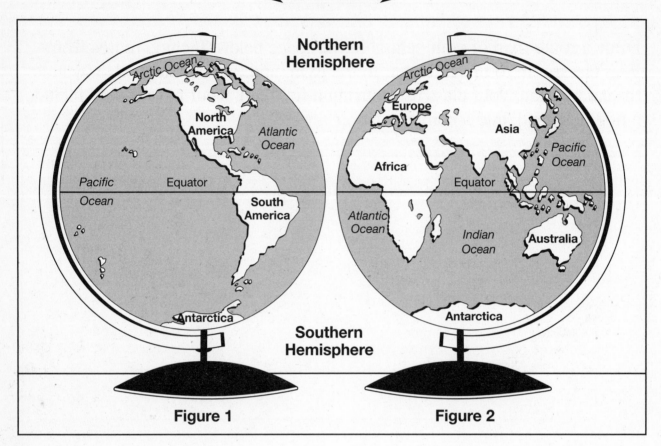

Figure 1

Figure 2

One of the most important lines on the globe is the **Equator**. The Equator is an imaginary line that goes around the middle of Earth. Study Figure 1 and Figure 2. Find the Equator on both sides of the globe.

The Equator divides the globe into two halves. Each half is called a **hemisphere**. Half the globe north of the Equator is the **Northern Hemisphere**. Half the globe south of the Equator is the **Southern Hemisphere**.

1. Look at Figure 1.

Find the land in the Northern Hemisphere. Circle it.

Find the land in the Southern Hemisphere. Circle it.

2. Look at Figure 2.

One continent is both north and south of the Equator.

What is the name of that continent?

_____

Name _____ Date _____

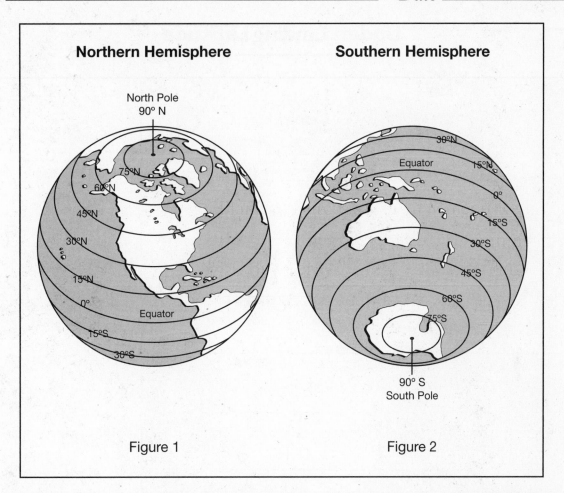

Figure 1

Figure 2

You can find places on globes and maps by using lines of **latitude**. The Equator is the most important line of latitude. The other lines of latitude measure distance north and south of the Equator.

All lines of latitude are numbered. The Equator is marked with a zero. It is 0° latitude. The sign ° stands for **degrees.** The lines that are farther away from the Equator have higher degree numbers. The North Pole is 90° north of the Equator. The South Pole is 90° south of the Equator. The North Pole and the South Pole have the highest degree numbers.

1. Find 60° North latitude in Figure 1. What continents does it cross?

_____

2. Find 15° South latitude in Figure 2. What continent does it cross?

_____

Maps: Read, Understand, Apply 3–4, SV9781419099427

Name _____ Date _____

Understanding Latitude

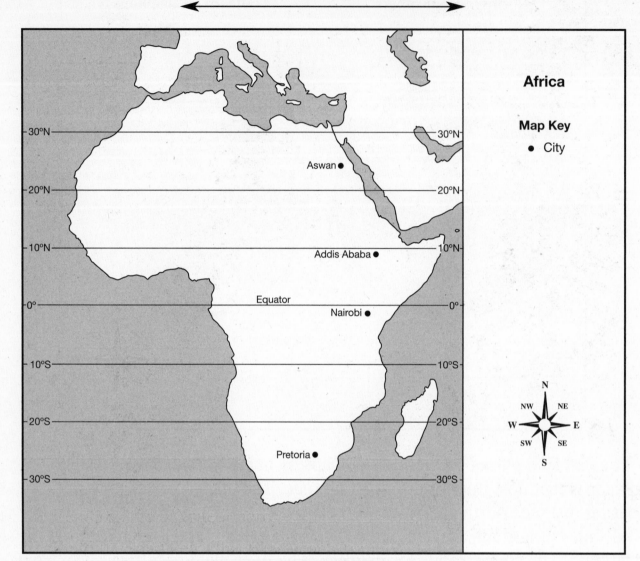

1. Color Africa green between 20°N and 30°N.

   What city lies in that area? _____

2. Color Africa brown between 0° and 10°N.

   What city lies in that area? _____

3. Color Africa yellow between 0° and 10°S.

   What city lies in that area? _____

4. Color Africa orange between 20°S and 30°S.

   What city lies in that area? _____

Name _____ Date _____

Cities on Lines of Latitude

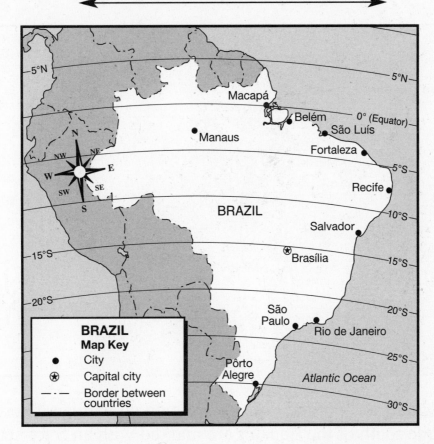

Sometimes a place falls between two lines of latitude. Then you must estimate its line of latitude. For example, look at the city of Salvador on the map of Brazil. Salvador is between 10°S and 15°S.

1. What city is located on the Equator? _____

2. What is the latitude of the capital city? Estimate your answer. _____

3. What city has latitude of 30°S? _____

4. What two cities are between 20°S and 25°S? _____

5. What city is about 8°S? _____

6. What is the latitude of Salvador? Estimate your answer. _____

Cities on Lines of Latitude
Maps: Read, Understand, Apply 3–4, SV9781419099427

Name _____ Date _____

Finding Latitude

←——————————————————→

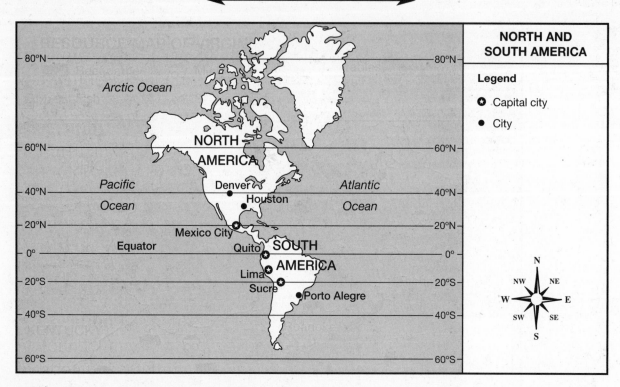

Degrees of latitude north of the Equator are marked with an N for north. Degrees of latitude south of the Equator are marked with an S for south.

1. Find the Equator. Trace it in red.

What city lies on the Equator? _____

2. Find 20°N. Trace that line of latitude in green.

What city lies at 20°N? _____

3. Find 20°S. Trace that line of latitude in orange.

What city lies at 20°S? _____

4. Fine 40°N. Trace that line of latitude in yellow.

What city lies at 40°N? _____

5. Find Houston on the map. Circle it in green.
Houston lies halfway between 20°N and 40°N.

Houston lies on what line of latitude? Make an estimate. _____

6. Find Lima on the map. Circle it in red.

Lima lies on what line of latitude? Make an estimate. _____

»»»»»»»»»»»»»»»»»»»»»»»»»»»»»»»»»»»»»»

Name _____ Date _____

Finding Latitude on a World Map

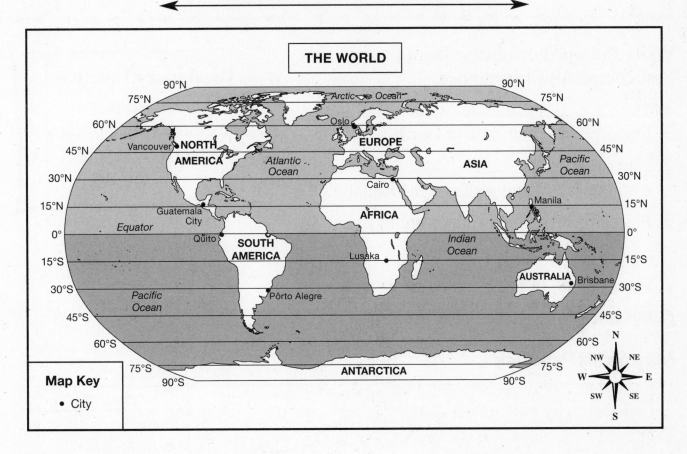

1. What two cities are at 30°S? _____

2. What two cities are at 15°N? _____

3. What city is at 30°N? _____

4. What city is near 45°N? _____

5. What city is at 60°N? _____

6. What city is at 0°? _____

7. 75°S crosses which continent? _____

8. What direction would you go from Guatemala City to Oslo? _____

9. What direction would you go from Cairo to Pôrto Alegre? _____

10. What direction would you go from Manila to Oslo? _____

Name _____ Date _____

Practice Your Skills

Write the word or phrase from the box that best completes the sentence.

Vocabulary Practice
latitude   Equator
Northern Hemisphere
Southern Hemisphere
degrees

1. The _____ is an imaginary line around the middle of Earth.

2. Lines of _____ measure distance north and south of the Equator.

3. Places north of the Equator are in the _____.

4. Places south of the Equator are in the _____.

5. Distances on a globe are measured in _____.

Map Skills Practice

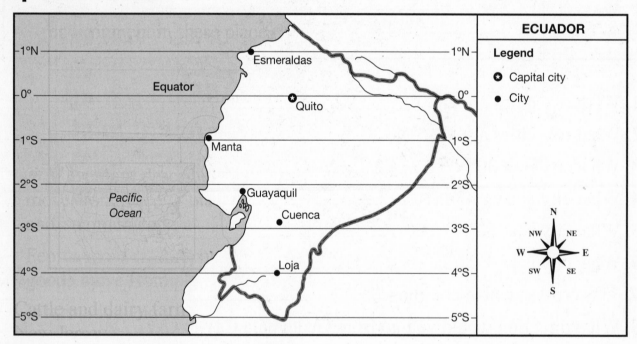

6. Find 1°S. What city lies near 1°S? _____

7. Find 1°N. What city lies at 1°N? _____

8. Find 4°S. What city lies at 4°S? _____

9. Find 2°S. What city lies near 2°S? _____

Name _____ Date _____

Following My Line of Latitude

Select a line of latitude on a map or globe and follow it for its full length. List all countries, landforms, bodies of water, and major cities on that line of latitude.

Line of Latitude

_____

Items located on this line of latitude

_____

_____

_____

_____

_____

_____

_____

Longitude

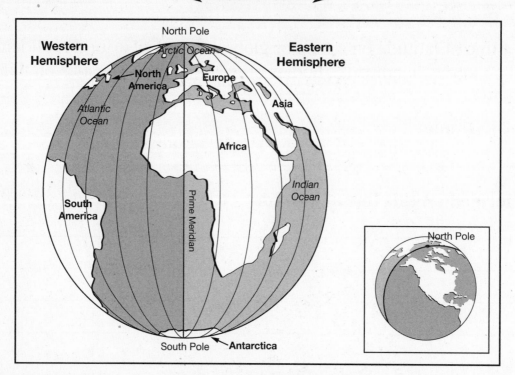

Another important line on the globe is the **Prime Meridian**. It is an imaginary line that goes from the North Pole to the South Pole.

Find the Prime Meridian in both pictures above. The Prime Meridian divides the globe into two hemispheres. Half the globe east of the Prime Meridian is the **Eastern Hemisphere**. Half the globe west of the Prime Meridian is the **Western Hemisphere**.

1. Find the land in the Eastern Hemisphere. Color it green.

2. What continents are in the Eastern Hemisphere?

_____

3. What oceans are in the Eastern Hemisphere?

_____

4. Find the land in the Western Hemisphere. Color it brown.

5. What five continents can you see in the Western Hemisphere?

_____

6. What oceans do you see in the Western Hemisphere?

_____

Maps: Read, Understand, Apply 3–4, SV9781419099427

Name _____   Date _____

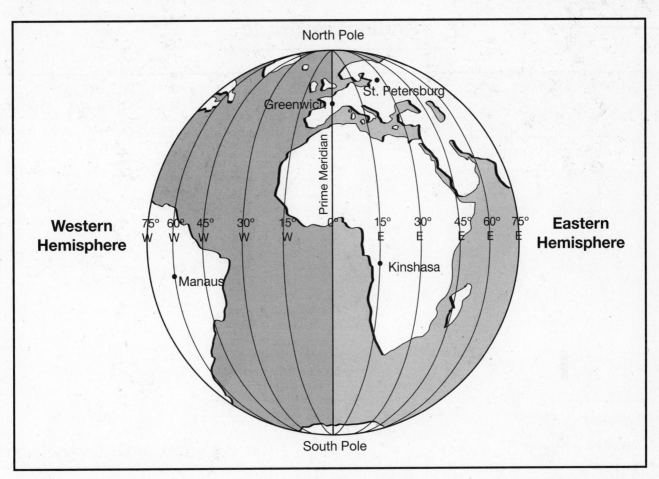

Find the Prime Meridian on the globe above. Now find the curved lines on each side of the Prime Meridian. These are called lines of **longitude**. Why are these lines curved?

We use lines of longitude to locate places east and west of the Prime Meridian. The lines are numbered and marked by degrees. The symbol ° stands for degrees. The Prime Meridian is at 0° longitude.

1. Find the 15°E longitude line. Trace it in blue.

2. What does the letter **E** stand for? _____

3. What city is at 15°E? _____

4. Find the 60°W longitude line. Trace it in orange.

5. What does the letter **W** stand for? _____

6. What city is at 60°W? _____

Maps: Read, Understand, Apply 3–4, SV9781419099427

Name _____   Date _____

Finding Longitude

⟷

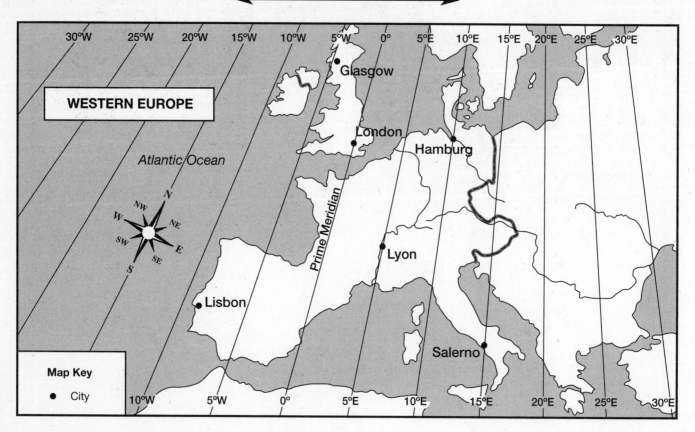

1. Find the Prime Meridian. Trace it in red.

What city lies on the Prime Meridian? _____

2. Find 5°W. Trace that line of longitude in green.

What city lies near 5°W? _____

3. Find 5°E. Trace that line of longitude in orange.

What city lies at 5°E? _____

4. Find 10°E. Trace that line of longitude in yellow.

What city lies at 10°E? _____

5. Find 10°W. Trace that line of longitude in purple.

What city lies near 10°W? _____

6. Find 15°E. Trace that line of longitude in brown.

What city lies at 15°E? _____

Finding Longitude
Maps: Read, Understand, Apply 3–4, SV9781419099427

Name _____   Date _____

Cities on Lines of Longitude

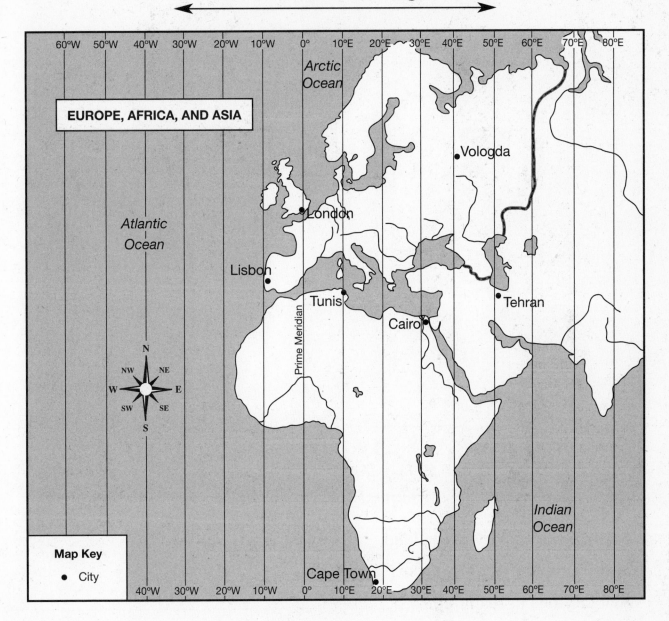

1. What city lies on the Prime Meridian? _____

2. What city lies at 10°E? _____

3. What city lies near 10°W? _____

4. What city lies near 20°E? _____

5. What city lies near 30°E? _____

6. What city lies near 40°E? _____

7. What city lies near 50°E? _____

Cities on Lines of Longitude
Maps: Read, Understand, Apply 3–4, SV9781419099427

Name _____ Date _____

Between Lines of Longitude

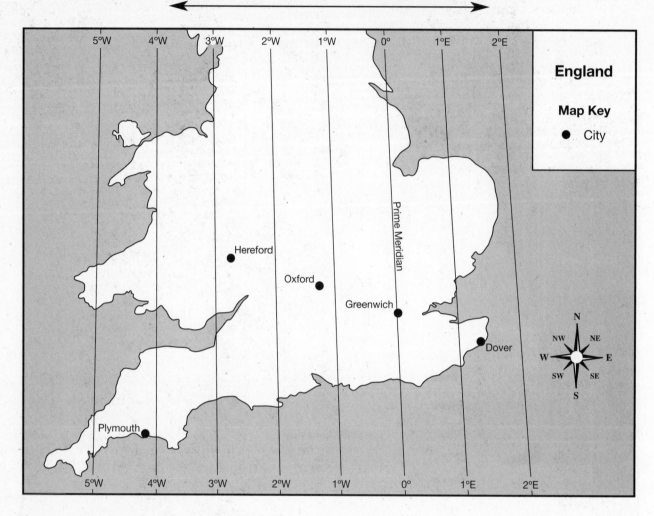

This map shows part of England.

1. Color England green between 1°E and 2°E.

What city lies in that area? _____

2. Color England brown between 1°W and 2°W.

What city lies in that area? _____

3. Color England yellow between 2°W and 3°W.

What city lies in that area? _____

4. Color England orange between 4°W and 5°W.

What city lies in that area? _____

5. What city lies on the Prime Meridian? _____

Maps: Read, Understand, Apply 3–4, SV9781419099427

Latitude and Longitude

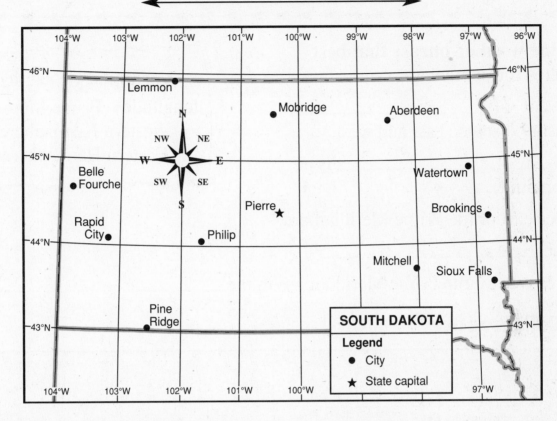

You have learned that lines of latitude run east and west around Earth. Lines of longitude run north and south. Together, the lines of latitude and longitude form a grid on maps and globes. By using lines of latitude and longitude, you can find any place on Earth.

Look at the map of South Dakota. Rapid City and Philip are both near 44°N latitude. Of course, they are not in the same place. By adding the longitude of each place, you can show exactly where it is. The latitude of a place is written first. The longitude is written next to it. Look at Watertown. We can say that Watertown is near 45°N, 97°W.

1. What city in South Dakota is located closest to 46°N, 102°W?

_____

2. What city in South Dakota is located near 44°N, 98°W? _____

3. What is the approximate latitude and longitude of the capital city of

South Dakota? _____

4. What is the line of latitude for Pine Ridge? _____

Practice Your Skills

Write the word or phrase that best completes the sentence.

1. Lines of _____ measure distance east and west.

2. The _____ is at 0° longitude.

3. Places east of the Prime Meridian are in the _____.

4. Places west of the Prime Meridian are in the _____.

> ## Vocabulary Practice
> longitude   Prime Meridian
> Western Hemisphere
> Eastern Hemisphere

Map Skills Practice

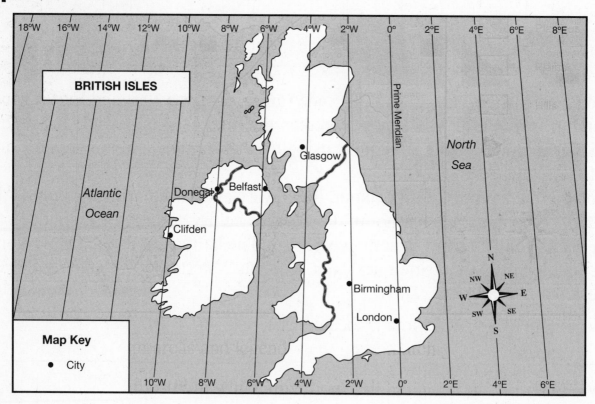

5. Find 2°W. What city lies at 2°W? _____

6. Find 0°. What city lies at 0°? _____

7. Find 6°W. What city lies near 6°W? _____

Name _____   Date _____

My Latitude and Longitude Game

Create a game to play with a partner using lines of latitude and longitude. Find cities on a map or globe and write their names and locations on the lines below.

City   **Location**

_____   _____

_____   _____

_____   _____

_____   _____

_____   _____

Once you have a list of cities, challenge your partner by asking him or her to find the cities on a map or globe based only on locations. Keep track of how many times your partner answers correctly.

My Latitude and Longitude Game
Maps: Read, Understand, Apply 3–4, SV9781419099427

Name _____ Date _____

Geography Theme: Location

Location describes where places are found. The map below shows Gabon, a country in Africa. Lines of latitude have been added to the map.

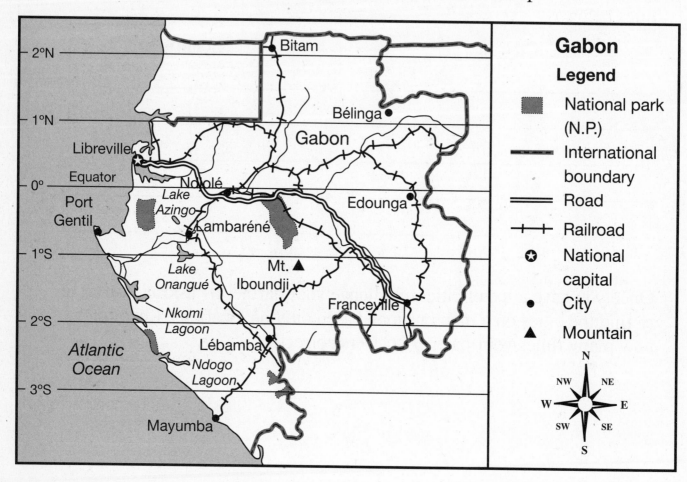

1. Find the Equator (0°) on the map. Trace it in red. What cities are located nearest to the Equator?

_____

2. What point of interest is located between 0° and 2°S latitude?

_____

Name _____   Date _____

The map below shows the countries of Portugal and Spain. Lines of longitude have been added to the map.

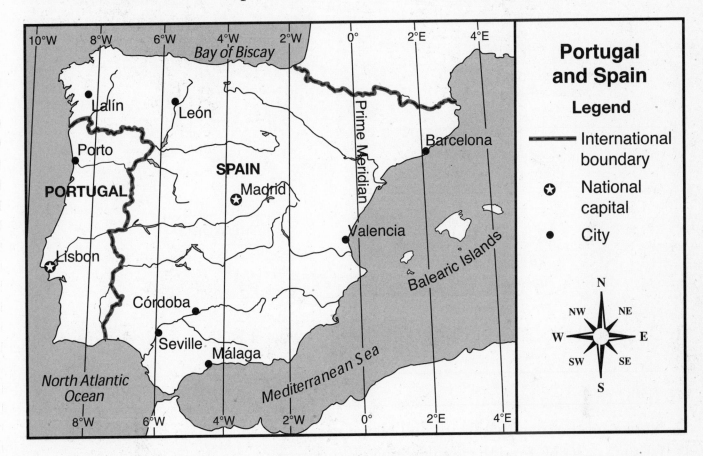

1. What line of longitude is nearest to Madrid, Spain?

_____

2. Find the capital of Portugal. Name this city and the line of longitude it is near.

_____

3. Which city in Spain is located near 8°W longitude?

_____

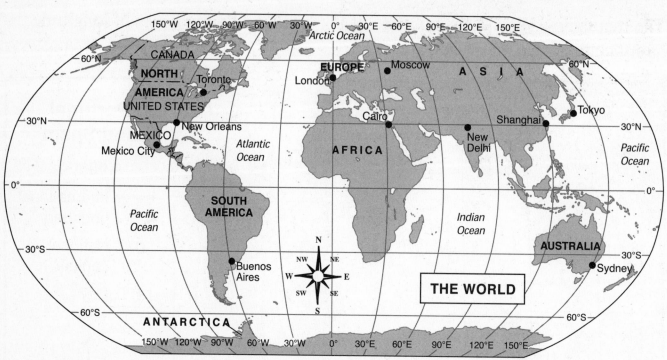

1. Describe the location of North America. Tell what it is near or what is around it.

_____

_____

2. Notice on the map that Cairo and New Orleans are located on the same line of latitude—30°N. Find these two cities on the map. Circle them.

3. Cairo and New Orleans, however, are not located at the same place because they are located on different lines of longitude. To give the exact location of a place, you must give both the latitude and the longitude. We say that the exact location of Cairo is 30°N, 30°E. What is the exact location of New Orleans?

_____

4. What is the exact location of Shanghai?

_____

Name _____ Date _____

You can tell the location of something by naming what is near it or what is around it. You also can tell the location by using an address, or numbers and a street name.

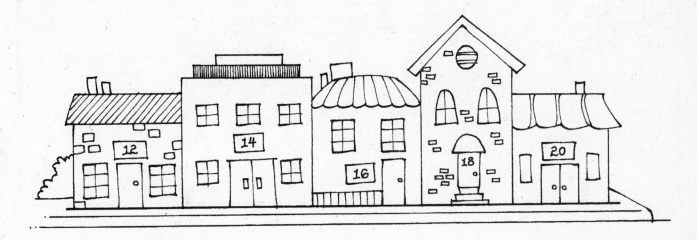

Answer the questions.

1. What makes it possible for the mail to get to the right home or business?

_____

2. What is your home address?

_____

_____

_____

3. What is your home near?

_____

_____

Geography Theme: Location
Maps: Read, Understand, Apply 3–4, SV9781419099427

Name _____   Date _____

Final Assessment

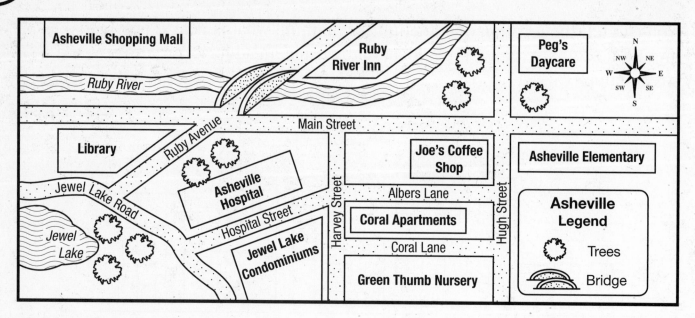

Use the map of Asheville to answer the questions.

1. Which direction is the Asheville Hospital from the Green Thumb Nursery?

   _____

2. Find the symbol for trees in the legend. How many trees are shown on the

   map? _____

3. You live at the Jewel Lake Condominiums and work at Joe's Coffee Shop.

   Which direction is your job from your home? _____

4. What landform is north of the library? _____

Use the map of Asheville to circle the correct answers.

5. You walk from the Asheville Shopping Mall to the Jewel Lake Condominiums.
   Which place would you pass taking Ruby Avenue to Jewel Lake Road?
   a. Coral Apartments   **c.** Green Thumb Nursery
   b. Asheville Hospital   **d.** Asheville Elementary

6. Which street runs northeast to southwest?
   a. Coral Lane   **c.** Hugh Street
   b. Hospital Street   **d.** Jewel Lake Road

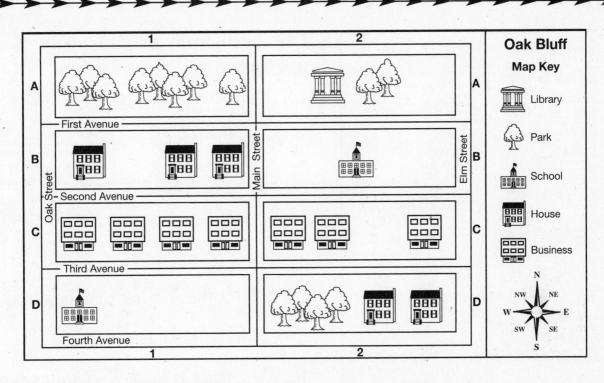

Use the grid map of Oak Bluff to answer the questions.

7. How many schools are there in Oak Bluff? _____

8. Which direction is the library from the school in the southwest corner of Oak Bluff? _____

9. On the map of Oak Bluff, the tree is the symbol for what place? _____

10. In which grid square is the library located? _____

Use the grid map of Oak Bluff to circle the correct answers.

11. The corner where Elm Street meets Third Avenue is which direction from the houses on Second Avenue?
    a. north
    b. west
    c. southeast
    d. southwest

12. A school is located southeast of the corner where which two streets meet?
    a. Oak Street and Second Avenue
    b. Main Street and First Avenue
    c. Elm Street and Fourth Avenue
    d. Main Street and Oak Street

Name _____   Date _____

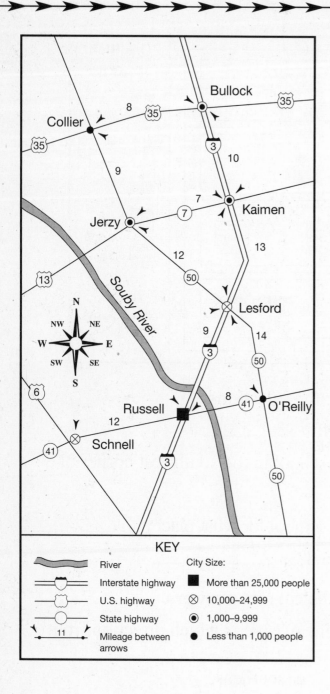

KEY

~~~~~~~ River

⎓ Interstate highway

◯ U.S. highway

◯ State highway

➤ 11 ➤ Mileage between arrows

City Size:

■ More than 25,000 people

⊗ 10,000–24,999

◉ 1,000–9,999

● Less than 1,000 people

Use the highway map to answer the questions.

13. Which two state highways do not cross the river? _____

_____

14. What is the only interstate highway shown on the map? _____

15. What is the shortest distance from Collier to Kaimen? _____

16. Which city is located 12 miles east and 9 miles northeast of Schnell?

_____

Use the highway map to circle the correct answers.

17. In what general direction does State Highway 50 run?
    a. north to south
    b. northwest to east
    c. northwest to southeast
    d. southwest to northeast

18. What is the population of Jerzy?
    a. below 1,000
    b. 1,000–9,999
    c. 10,000–24,999
    d. above 25,000

Final Assessment
Maps: Read, Understand, Apply 3–4, SV9781419099427

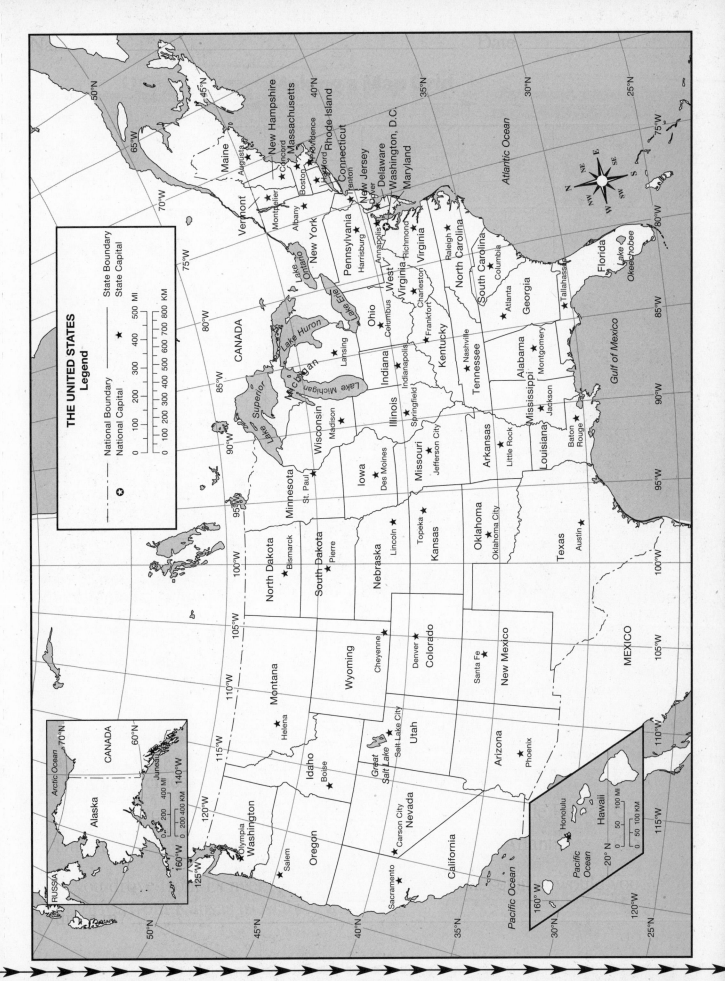

THE UNITED STATES

Legend

National Boundary ⎯ State Boundary

National Capital ⊛ State Capital ★

Atlas: United States
Maps: Read, Understand, Apply 3–4, SV9781419099427

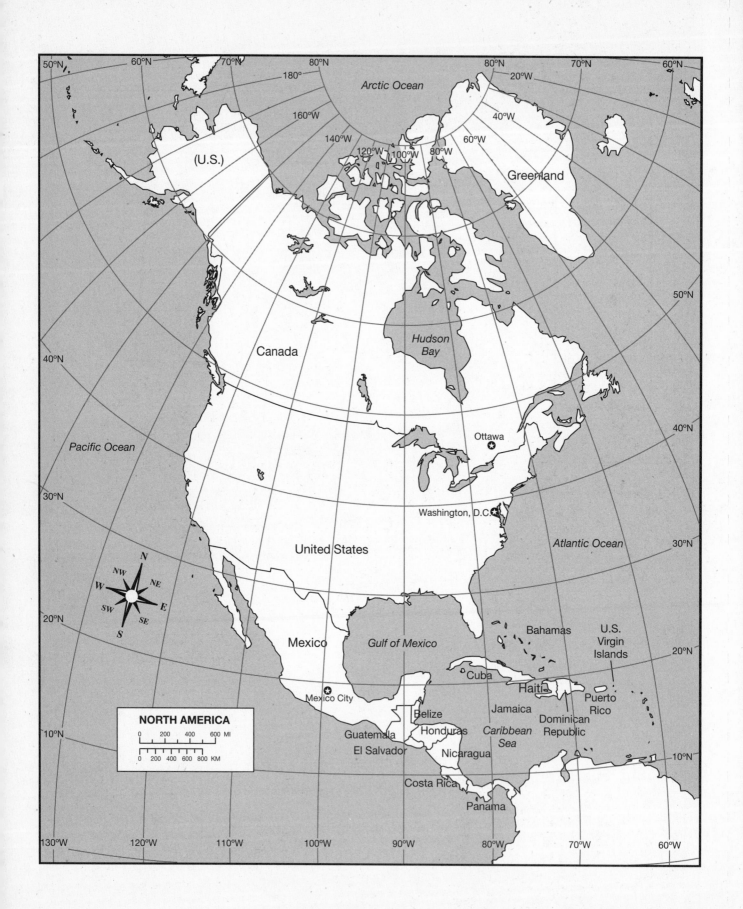

NORTH AMERICA

0   200   400   600 MI
0   200 400 600 800 KM

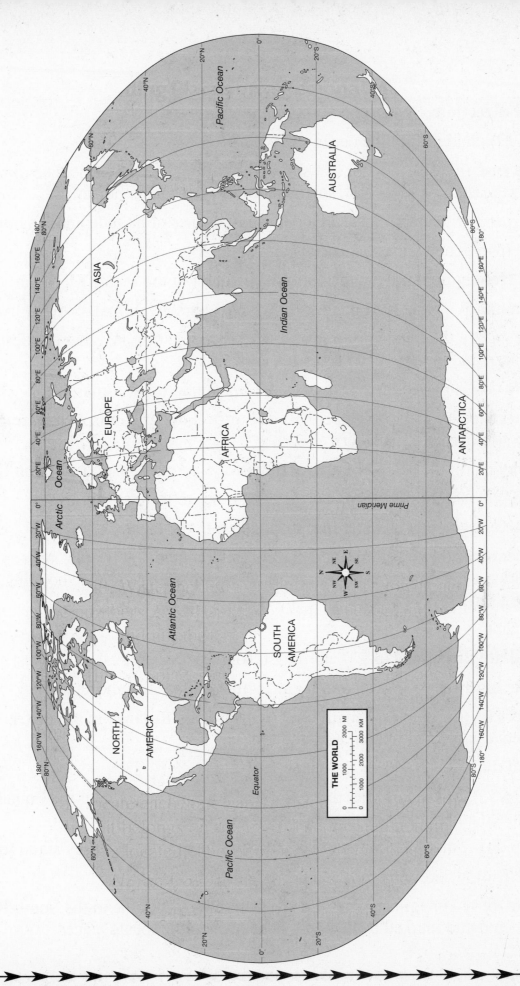

THE WORLD

Atlas: The World
Maps: Read, Understand, Apply 3–4, SV9781419099427

Glossary

cardinal directions (p. 14) north, south, east, and west

coast (p. 42) land next to the ocean

compass rose (p. 14) a symbol that shows the cardinal and intermediate directions: north, northeast, east, southeast, south, southwest, west, and northwest

degrees (p. 83) the unit of measurement used for lines of latitude and longitude

distance (p. 62) how far one place is from another

Eastern Hemisphere (p. 90) the half of Earth east of the Prime Meridian

environment (p. 7) the surroundings in which a person, animal, or plant lives

Equator (p. 82) the imaginary line around the middle of Earth that divides Earth into the Northern and Southern Hemispheres

factory (p. 34) a place where resources are made into other things

hemisphere (p. 82) half the globe; half of Earth; the four hemispheres are Eastern, Western, Northern, and Southern

geography (p. 6) the study of Earth and the ways people live and work on Earth

grid (p. 54) a pattern of lines that cross each other to form squares

gulf (p. 42) large body of water that cuts deep into the land

human features (p. 6) features of a place or region made by people, such as buildings, roads, parks, playgrounds, bridges, railroads, farms, factories, and shopping malls

human/environment interaction (p. 7) the ways people live with and change their environment

intermediate directions (p. 23) northeast, southeast, southwest, northwest

interstate highway (p. 74) a main highway that crosses the entire country

kilometers (p. 62) a unit of length used in measuring distance in the metric system. Kilometers can also be written KM and km.

landform map (p. 42) shows the shape of the land

latitude (p. 83) imaginary lines that circle Earth north and south of the Equator. They are numbered and marked by degrees. They are used to locate places.

legend (p. 14) a map key, or list of symbols on a map and what they stand for

location (p. 6) where something on Earth is found

longitude (p. 91) imaginary lines that go from the North Pole to the South Pole. They are numbered and marked by degrees. They are used to locate places.

map (p. 14) a drawing of a real place that shows the place from above

map index (p. 55) the alphabetical list of places on a map with their grid squares

map key (p. 14) the guide that tells what the symbols on a map stand for

map scale (p. 62) the guide that tells what the distances on a map stand for

miles (p. 62) a unit of length used in measuring distance. Miles can also be written MI or mi.

movement (p. 8) how people, goods, information, and ideas move from place to place through transportation and communication

natural resources (p. 6) things in nature that people can use, such as water, trees, oil, and gold

Northern Hemisphere (p. 82) the half of Earth north of the Equator

physical features (p. 6) features of a place or region formed by nature, such as bodies of water, landforms, climate, natural resources, and plants and animals

place (p. 6) tells about the physical and human features of an area that make it different from other areas

plain (p. 42) a large area of flat land

plateau (p. 42) an area of high, flat land

population (p. 18) the number of people who live in a place

Prime Meridian (p. 90) the line of longitude running from the South Pole to the North Pole and measured at 0°. It helps divide Earth into the Eastern and Western Hemispheres.

regions (p. 9) areas that share one or more features

resources (p. 34) things people can use. Some resources are oil, lumber, or water.

route (p. 74) a road or path from one place to another. Highways, railroads, waterways, and trails are routes.

Southern Hemisphere (p. 82) the half of Earth south of the Equator

state highway (p. 74) a main road that connects cities and towns within the boundaries of one state

symbol (p. 14) a picture on a map that stands for something real

title (p. 14) the name of a map

U.S. highway (p. 74) a main highway that passes through more than one state

Western Hemisphere (p. 90) the half of Earth west of the Prime Meridian

Answer Key

Pages 6–9
1. Answers will vary.
2. Answers may include: buildings, the Gateway Arch.
3. Answers may include: the waterfall, rocks, mountains, trees.
4. Answers may include: differences in weather, temperature, and terrain that would result in wearing different clothes, growing different crops, or having different jobs.
5. Answers may include: to build houses and to connect land separated by water.
6. Information and ideas are moving through the computer and between the students.
7. Answers may include: because of the physical feature of the mountains or because of the climate or animal life found in the mountains.

Page 10
1. Ensure that students circle Ana's house.
2. streets, bike path, railroad
3. Elm Street, Long Road, Oak Street
4. Elm Street, Long Road

Page 11
1. New City
2. daily newspapers, library, cable TV station
3. Field City
4. Accept all reasonable answers.

Page 12
1. railroad and highway
2. Albuquerque, because it has an airport, railroad, and major highway.
3. Highway 25
4. Socorro, Albuquerque, Rio Rancho

Page 13
1. a, b
2. a, b
3. d
4. c
5. a, d
6. a, b
7. d
8. c
9. a
10. d

Page 14
1. Dana's Neighborhood

2. Answers may include: hospital, house, school, river.
3. Answers may include: Ranch Road (N), Green River (E), Maple Drive (S), school (W).

Page 15
1. east
2. south
3. north
4. west

Page 16
1. Ben Franklin's Neighborhood
2. Ensure compass is correctly circled.
3. south
4. north
5. Norris House
6. Ben Franklin's House

Page 17
1. McDonald Park
2. Ensure that all symbols in the legend and on the map are checked.
3. Ensure that the north arrow is circled.
For questions 4–8, ensure that items are drawn to match directions.

Page 18
1. Ensure that the pattern drawn matches the pattern for *Many people* on the map and legend.
2. San Francisco
3. many
4. many
5. Answers may include: to find jobs or to live close to a large body of water.

Page 19
1. Merrimac River
2. Washington, D.C.
3. Buffalo
4. Canada and United States of America
5. Maine
6. Hudson River

Page 20
1. map
2. symbol
3. legend
4. compass rose
5. cardinal directions
6. Hunger Mountain
7. Worcester
8. Springfield
9. Holyoke

Page 21
Maps will vary.

Page 23
1. a. NW
   b. NE
   c. NW
2. a. SW
   b. SE
   c. NE

Page 24
1. Illinois
2. Ensure that the intermediate direction arrows are correctly labeled.
For questions 3-6, ensure that lines are drawn to match directions.
3. Ensure that Springfield is circled; northeast
4. southwest
5. southeast
6. northwest

Page 25
1. northwest
2. southeast
3. north, east
4. south, west
5. northwest
6. southeast
7. southwest
8. northeast

Page 26
1. Ensure that the intermediate direction arrows are correctly labeled.
2. Ensure that Phoenix is circled.
3. northwest
4. southeastern
5. southwestern
6. northwest
7. northeastern
8. southeast

Page 27
For questions 1–3, ensure that items are colored to match directions.
4. a. E
   b. SE
   c. SW
   d. S
   e. N
   f. W
   g. SE
   h. NW

Page 28
1. Intermediate
2. Ensure that the intermediate direction arrows are correctly labeled.
3. Ensure that Lanai is circled.
For questions 4–6, ensure that lines are drawn to match directions.
4. east
5. southeast
6. northwest
7. a. Mauna Loa
   b. Mauna Kea

Page 29
Answers and maps will vary.

Page 30
1. clothing store
2. Answers may include: movie theater, food court, parking areas, outdoor gardens, fountain, statue
3. Ensure that the toy store is circled and labeled with an *H*.

Page 31
1. Ensure that the fairgrounds are circled and labeled with an *H*.
2. Answers may include: Bear Lake or the beach. Ensure that the feature is labeled with a *P*.
3. Accept all reasonable answers.

Page 32
1. Ensure that the map is correctly labeled.
2. Answers may include: Potomac River or Anacostia River.
3. Ensure that the capitol is circled and labeled with an *H*.
4. Answers may include: National Zoological Park, Walter Reed Army Medical Center, Catholic University of America, American University, U.S. Naval Observatory, Howard University, Union Station, Jefferson Memorial, Washington Monument, Lincoln Memorial, or White House.

Page 33
1. Ensure that the map is correctly labeled.
2. Answers may include: Rampart Cave, Kanab Plateau, Coconino Plateau, Kaibab Plateau, Shivwits Plateau, Point Imperial, North Rim, South Rim, Granite Rapids, canyons, Kanab Creek
3. Ensure that the Grand Canyon Village is circled.
4. Answers may include: ranger stations, hiking trails, or campgrounds
5. Answers will vary.

Page 34
1. Resources in California
2. Answers may include: factories, dairy, and fish.
3. north: lumber; south: fish, oil, fruit, and mining

Page 36
1. Resources in California
2. Ensure that all symbols in the legend and on the map are checked.
3. Ensure that the north arrow is circled.
For questions 4–7, ensure that items are drawn to match directions.

Page 37
1. Resources in Texas
2. Austin
For questions 3–6, ensure that items are drawn to match directions.
7. **a.** cotton **b.** cattle **c.** oil

Page 38
1. Resource Map of Virginia
2. western
3. mining, cattle
4. fish
5. soybeans

Page 39
1. Resources in Florida
2. Ensure Florida is circled on the small map; southern United States
3. northeast
4. southeast
5. Miami, St. Petersburg
6. fish, fruit, vegetables

Page 40
1. resource
2. factory
3. northwestern
4. vegetables
5. **a.** dairy
   b. fruit
   c. vegetables
6. factories

Page 41
Maps will vary.

Page 43
1. plateaus, hills, plains
2. rivers
3. western
4. central U.S.
5. mountains
6. Ensure that the gulf label is circled on both maps.

Page 44
1. Landforms in the United States
2. Ensure that the intermediate direction arrows are circled.

3.–4. Ensure that items are colored to match directions.
5. Answers will vary.

Page 45
1. Landforms in the United States
2. Ensure that the east direction arrow is circled.
3. Los Angeles
4. New York City, Charleston
5. Biloxi, New Orleans
6. Duluth, Milwaukee, Buffalo
7. Denver, Cheyenne
8. New Orleans, St. Paul, St. Louis

Page 46
1. Alaska Landforms
2. Ensure that the south direction arrow is circled.
3. plains
4. mountains
5. plains
6. hills

Page 47
1.–2. Ensure that items are colored to match directions.
3. west
4. east
5. Lake Erie, Lake Ontario
6. plains
7. plains

Page 48
1. plateau
2. gulf
3. coast
4. Ensure that items are colored to match directions.
5. west
6. east
7. Lake Erie
8. Ohio River

Page 49
Answers will vary.

Page 50
1. forests, grasslands, desert plants
2. forests
3. grasslands; Ensure that the Missouri River is circled correctly.
4. desert plants

Page 51
1. Ensure that tennis courts are correctly labeled.
2. southwest
3. crafts
4. All parks in Park City have the same features.

Page 52
Answers will vary.

Page 53
Mountains: goat, lion, bighorn sheep
Deserts: fox, lizard, kangaroo rat
Plains: buffalo, harvest mouse, pronghorn

Page 54
1. A, B, C, D
2. 1, 2, 3, 4
3. Ensure square C-3 is circled.
4. B-4
5. A-1, B-1, C-1, D-1

Page 55
1. D-1   2. D-3

Page 56
1. **a.** A-4   **d.** B-2
   b. C-2   **e.** A-2
   c. C-3   **f.** B-4
2. C-2, B-2, C-3
3. **a.** NE   **c.** W
   b. NW   **d.** S

Page 57
1. Ensure that the map grid is labeled to match directions.
2. **a.** B-6   **d.** D-6
   b. C-4   **e.** C-2
   c. B-3   **f.** B-4
3. Ensure that all cities are correctly labeled.
4. B-3, B-4, B-5, B-6

Page 58
1. Kansas
2. Ensure that the intermediate direction arrows are correctly labeled.
3. 4, 8
4. Topeka
5. Mt. Sunflower
6. Wichita
7. Arkansas River
8. Great Bend (C-4), Dodge City (D-3), or Wichita (D-5)

Page 59
1. Ensure that the map grid is labeled to match directions.
2. **a.** South Dakota
   b. Nebraska
   c. Iowa
   d. North Dakota
3. **a.** North Dakota
   b. Missouri
   c. South Dakota
   d. Iowa
   e. Nebraska
   f. Kansas

Page 60
1. grid
2. index
3. Raleigh; A-5
4. **a.** Asheville
   b. B-3
   c. B-5

d. Lake Hickory
e. A-7
f. C-5
g. C-6
h. Winston-Salem

Page 61
Answers will vary.

Page 62
1. MI   2. KM

Page 64
1. The Denver Area
2. Ensure that all symbols in the legend and on the map are checked.
3. Ensure that the intermediate direction arrows are labeled.
4. 3
5. 6
6. $8\frac{1}{2}$
7. $4\frac{1}{2}$
8. 12

Page 65
For questions 1–4, ensure that lines are drawn to match directions.
1. about 225   4. about 105
2. about 140   5. about 555
3. about 85

Page 66
1. 850   5. 1,100
2. 1,700   6. 1,700
3. 1,250   7. 900
4. 700

Page 67
Day 2: southwest, about 350
Day 3: southeast, about 230
Day 4: north, about 175
Day 5: northwest, about 350

Page 68
1. Distance   5. miles
2. map scale   6. 40
3. distance   7. 80
4. kilometers

Page 69
Maps will vary.

Page 70
1. in the northwest and along the northern, southern, and eastern boundaries
2. in the western, northeastern, southeastern, and central parts
3. far southwest and far northeast corners of the state
4. Accept all reasonable answers.

Page 71
1. The factory polluted Lake Ellyn and killed fish.

Maps: Read, Understand, Apply 3–4, SV9781419099427

2. Ensure events were correctly inserted.
3. Answers will vary.

Page 72
1. for farming
2. fishing
3. Answers will vary.

Page 73
1. Humans changed the environment by destroying the forest. Answers may include: animal life was destroyed, or erosion may occur because the trees have been cut down.
2. They are trying to save and protect the environment by planting trees that can hold the soil in place and provide homes for some animals.

Page 74
1. 5, 15, 35, 95
2. 20, 93, 83, 82
3. 33 (CA), 23 (MN), 114 (TX), 17 (NY), 20 (FL)

Page 75
1. 59   4. 101
2. 130   5. 133
3. 32

Page 76
1. Routes in central Mississippi
2. interstate highway, U.S. highway, state highway
3. Ensure that the intermediate direction arrows are labeled.
4. Interstate 20
5. U.S. 49
6. Yazoo City and Tchula
7. Ensure that Carthage is labeled correctly.
8. U.S. 51

Page 77
1. 40, 25, 10
2. Santa Fe
3. U.S. highway
4. southeast, 70 miles
5. Albuquerque, Las Cruces

Page 78
1. Routes in Texas
2. a. 72   3. a. 415
   b. 200   b. 598
   c. 150   c. 572
   d. 237   d. 558

Page 79
1. a. Key West to Long Key: 65
   b. Jupiter to Boca Raton: 45
   c. Ft. Lauderdale to Miami Beach: 22
2. 100
3. Key Largo
4. 239

Page 80
1. interstate highway
2. state highway
3. U.S. highway
4. route
5. Olympia, Tacoma, Seattle, Bellingham
6. U.S. 101
7. 20

Page 81
Maps will vary.

Page 82
1. Ensure that land in the Northern and Southern hemispheres is circled.
2. Africa

Page 83
1. North America, Europe, Asia
2. Australia

Page 84
For questions 1–4, ensure that select areas are colored correctly.
1. Aswan   3. Nairobi
2. Addis Ababa   4. Pretoria

Page 85
1. Macapá
2. 16°S
3. Pôrto Alegre
4. São Paulo, Rio de Janeiro
5. Recife
6. 13°S

Page 86
For questions 1–4, ensure that select lines of latitude are correctly colored.
1. Quito
2. Mexico City
3. Sucre
4. Denver
5. Ensure that Houston is circled in green; 30°N
6. Ensure that Lima is circled in red; 10°S

Page 87
1. Pôrto Alegre, Brisbane
2. Guatemala City, Manila
3. Cairo
4. Vancouver
5. Oslo
6. Quito
7. Antarctica
8. NE
9. SW
10. NW

Page 88
1. Equator
2. latitude
3. Northern Hemisphere
4. Southern Hemisphere

5. degrees
6. Manta
7. Esmeraldas
8. Loja
9. Guayaquil

Page 89
Answers will vary.

Page 90
1. Ensure that land in the Eastern Hemisphere is colored green.
2. Europe, Asia, Africa, Antarctica
3. Indian Ocean, Arctic Ocean
4. Ensure that land in the Western Hemisphere is colored brown.
5. North America, South America, Antarctica, Europe, Africa
6. Atlantic Ocean, Arctic Ocean

Page 91
1. Ensure that the 15°E longitude line is traced in blue.
2. east
3. Kinshasa
4. Ensure that the 60°W longitude line is traced in orange.
5. west
6. Manaus

Page 92
For questions 1–6, ensure that select lines of longitude are correctly colored.
1. London   4. Hamburg
2. Glasgow   5. Lisbon
3. Lyon   6. Salerno

Page 93
1. London   5. Cairo
2. Tunis   6. Vologda
3. Lisbon   7. Tehran
4. Cape Town

Page 94
For questions 1–4, ensure that map sections are colored to match directions.
1. Dover   4. Plymouth
2. Oxford   5. Greenwich
3. Hereford

Page 95
1. Lemmon
2. Mitchell
3. about 44°N, 100° W
4. 43°N

Page 96
1. longitude
2. Prime Meridian
3. Eastern Hemisphere

4. Western Hemisphere
5. Birmingham
6. London
7. Belfast

Page 97
Answers will vary.

Page 98
1. Ensure the Equator is traced; Ndjolé and Edounga
2. Any of the following: Lake Onangué, Nkomi Lagoon, Mt. Iboundji, Lake Azingo, national parks

Page 99
1. 4°W
2. Lisbon, 9°W
3. Lalín

Page 100
1. Answers may include: North America is north of South America, North America is west of the Atlantic Ocean, North America is north and east of the Pacific Ocean.
2. Ensure that cities are circled to match directions.
3. 30°N, 90°W
4. 30°N, 120°E

Page 101
1. an address
2. Answers will vary.
3. Answers will vary.

Pages 102–104
1. northwest
2. 8
3. northeast
4. Ruby River
5. b
6. b
7. 2
8. northeast
9. park
10. A-2
11. c
12. b
13. State Highway 7 and State Highway 50
14. Interstate 3
15. 16 miles
16. Lesford
17. c
18. b

Answer Key
Maps: Read, Understand, Apply 3–4, SV9781419099427